THE DURATION OF PREGNANCY.

EXPLANATION.—Find in the upper horizontal row the date of last menstruation; the figure beneath it shows the expiration of 280 days. Prepared by W. W. Ely, M.D. Published in the Medical Register. Presented with the

Compliments of HANCE BROTHERS & WHITE, Philadelphia.

Jan.	1	2	3	4	5	6	7	8	9	10	11	12	13	14	15	16	17	18	19	20	21	22	23	24	25	25	27	28	29	30	31	
Oct.	8	9	10	11	12	13	14	15	16	17	18	19	20	21	22	23	24	25	26	27	28	29	30	31	1	2	3	4	5	6	7	*Nov.*
Feb.	1	2	3	4	5	6	7	8	9	10	11	12	13	14	15	16	17	18	19	20	21	22	23	24	25	26	27	28				
Nov.	8	9	10	11	12	13	14	15	16	17	18	19	20	21	22	23	24	25	26	27	28	29	30	1	2	3	4	5				*Dec.*
March	1	2	3	4	5	6	7	8	9	10	11	12	13	14	15	16	17	18	19	20	21	22	23	24	25	26	27	28	29	30	31	
Dec.	6	7	8	9	10	11	12	13	14	15	16	17	18	19	20	21	22	23	24	25	26	27	28	29	30	31	1	2	3	4	5	*Jan.*
April	1	2	3	4	5	6	7	8	9	10	11	12	13	14	15	16	17	18	19	20	21	22	23	24	25	26	27	28	29	30		
Jan.	6	7	8	9	10	11	12	13	14	15	16	17	18	19	20	21	22	23	24	25	26	27	28	29	30	31	1	2	3	4		*Feb.*
May	1	2	3	4	5	6	7	8	9	10	11	12	13	14	15	16	17	18	19	20	21	22	23	24	25	26	27	28	29	30	31	
Feb.	5	6	7	8	9	10	11	12	13	14	15	16	17	18	19	20	21	22	23	24	25	26	27	28	1	2	3	4	5	6	7	*March.*
June	1	2	3	4	5	6	7	8	9	10	11	12	13	14	15	16	17	18	19	20	21	22	23	24	25	26	27	28	29	30		
March	8	9	10	11	12	13	14	15	16	17	18	19	20	21	22	23	24	25	26	27	28	29	30	31	1	2	3	4	5	6		*April.*
July	1	2	3	4	5	6	7	8	9	10	11	12	13	14	15	16	17	18	19	20	21	22	23	24	25	26	27	28	29	30	31	
April	7	8	9	10	11	12	13	14	15	16	17	18	19	20	21	22	23	24	25	26	27	28	29	30	1	2	3	4	5	6	7	*May.*
Aug.	1	2	3	4	5	6	7	8	9	10	11	12	13	14	15	16	17	18	19	20	21	22	23	24	25	26	27	28	29	30	31	
May	8	9	10	11	12	13	14	15	16	17	18	19	20	21	22	23	24	25	26	27	28	29	30	31	1	2	3	4	5	6	7	*June.*
Sept.	1	2	3	4	5	6	7	8	9	10	11	12	13	14	15	16	17	18	19	20	21	22	23	24	25	26	27	28	29	30		
June	8	9	10	11	12	13	14	15	16	17	18	19	20	21	22	23	24	25	26	27	28	29	30	1	2	3	4	5	6	7		*July.*
Oct.	1	2	3	4	5	6	7	8	9	10	11	12	13	14	15	16	17	18	19	20	21	22	23	24	25	26	27	28	29	30	31	
July	8	9	10	11	12	13	14	15	16	17	18	19	20	21	22	23	24	25	26	27	28	29	30	31	1	2	3	4	5	6	7	*Aug.*
Nov.	1	2	3	4	5	6	7	8	9	10	11	12	13	14	15	16	17	18	19	20	21	22	23	24	25	26	27	28	29	30		
Aug.	8	9	10	11	12	13	14	15	16	17	18	19	20	21	22	23	24	25	26	27	28	29	30	31	1	2	3	4	5	6		*Sept.*
Dec.	1	2	3	4	5	6	7	8	9	10	11	12	13	14	15	16	17	18	19	20	21	22	23	24	25	26	27	28	29	30	31	
Sept.	7	8	9	10	11	12	13	14	15	16	17	18	19	20	21	22	23	24	25	26	27	28	29	30	1	2	3	4	5	6	7	*Oct.*

Propert[illegible] [illegible]
C. Reagan
[illegible]

Inside Front Cover

Buncombe County, North Carolina Births

- 1858-1888 -

Journal
of
Dr. James Americus Reagan

Edited by:
William D. Bennett

Southern Historical Press, Inc.
Greenville, South Carolina

SOUTHERN HISTORICAL PRESS, INC.
PO BOX 1267
Greenville, SC 29601

ISBN #978-1-63914-072-5

Printed in the United States of America

INTRODUCTION

This volume is a reproduction of a journal kept by Dr. James Americus Reagan of Buncombe County, North Carolina. The following biography of Dr. Reagan is taken from Holston Methodism by R. N. Price.

"James Americus Reagan was born in Monroe County, Tenn., 20 October 1824. His parents were Presbyterians. He was reared in Cleveland, Tenn. There in an academy he was educated. He was licensed to preach in 1846. The same year he was admitted into the Holstein Conference (Methodist Episcopal Church, South) and appointed to Tazewell Circuit in Virginia. He located (retired from the itinerate ministry) in 1853 on account of ill health and studied medicine. He got his degree of M. D. from two medical schools, one of which was the Medical Department of Vanderbuilt University. He spent a useful life in the practice of medicine, getting an extensive practice and making a comfortable living. He never retired from active ministry, but did a great deal of preaching. He was especially in demand for funeral and memorial sermons. His long life was crowded with work. He was six years on the Medical Examining Board of North Carolina, three years President of the Buncombe County Medical Society, for some time a consulting physician of the Mission Hospital (in Asheville), eight years on the Buncombe County Board of Commissioners, for some years Treasurer of the Board of Finance in the Holston Conference and Secretary of the Board of Education, and for fifteen years on the Board of Education of the Western North Carolina Conference.

"Dr. Reagan always took pride in doing everything he undertook to do and do it thoroughly. He was laborious and painstaking. He was a careful reader, and read a number of standard Methodist works, besides an extensive course of medicine and regular issues of medical journals. He wrote much for the newspapers and medical journals. He received the degrees of A. M. and D. D. from Weaverville College. Dr. Reagan was a surgeon as well as a physician, and practiced surgery in four counties.

"Dr. Reagan was one of the founders of Weaverville College. Before and during the Civil War the Masonic and Temperance Hall at Reems Creek had been used for high school purposes. When the war was over the hall had burned, the negroes freed, and the money in the hands of the people was worthless. Dr. Reagan called the people together and suggested the erection of a college building. They agreed to the proposition and a brick building was erected and Weaverville College was chartered. Montraville Weaver gave the land and a part of the money. The principal contributors were John S. Weaver, William R. Baird, and Dr. Reagan.

"Dr. Reagan, who had been President of the Sons of Temperance High School, now became the first President of the college, and held this position until he was succeeded by Dr. James S. Kennedy. Weaverville College served the area until 1933 when it, and Rutherford College, merged with Brevard School for Girls to form present Brevard Junior College in Brevard, North Carolina.

"Dr. Reagan died at his home, in Weaverville, N. C., 24 October 1910, aged eighty six years and four days. He married, in 1851, to Miss Mary Weaver, daughter of Rev. Montraville Weaver; and she died in 1890. A few years later he married Miss Mary Parks, of Hillsboro, N. C., who lived only another year or two. He was married a third time to Mrs. Anne Nealy, a niece of Hon. Nicholas Woodfin, who survived Dr. Reagan. His children were all by his first marriage and were Mrs. T. H. Reeves, W. L. Reagan, J. J. Reagan, Mrs. C. A. Nichols, and Mrs. E. M. Goolsby. One son, J. A. Reagan, Jr., died in 1907."

The editor originally planned to transcribe this journal. However, Dr. Reagan used a number of medical terms which were totally unfamiliar to the editor. For fear of misreading these terms, which the editor felt would be meaningful to anyone connected with the family mentioned, it was decided to reproduce the original pages rather than provide a transcript. This journal contains the records of approximately 750 births which Dr. Reagan attended during the thirty years from late 1858 to late 1888. Dr. Reagan numbered each of his entries. On a few occasions he repeated a number and at one point skipped approximately thirty numbers. Turning the journal over and starting at the back, he recorded recipes of prescriptions for various disorders. Those pages which include no births have been reversed for ease in reading. This reproduction is the complete journal.

The editor wishes to thank Mr. George Stevenson for calling attention to this journal and Jo White Linn for her kind assistance in helping bring this volume to fruition.

Dr. J. A. Keagan = Record of Babies Delivered

Received practice in the Spring of 1858. The first case of midwifery which I attended was the 31st of August - the wife of James Frady. The labor was brought on prematurely by a fall. I found in her case "uvi ursa" better than "ergot". She was delivered after long suffering in about 48 hours - they both lived - mother & child - It was 7½ months from the best light I could get. Child a girl.

2 - Case - wife of W. B. Cheek - all right
Child a boy. = Sept. 8th '58

3 Case - Wife of W. A. Bridges - all right
Child a boy = Sept. 20th '58

4 Case. Jordan Lankford's wife - first child
small rent in perineum - no damage - all
did well Child a girl = Sept. 21st '58

5 Case. Wife of Wm. M. Weaver - Child
partly born when I got to her - all right
Child a girl. Sept. 25th '58

6 Case - a girl - wife of Rev. W. F. Parker
tolerably hard labor - hard to cleanse
did well.

7 Case a boy. A. M. Fox' wife - placenta
grown to lower part of womb - did well boy

8 Dec. 1858 Wife of James Atkin - had a midwife there. Hemorrhage commenced, and they sent for me. Child's head fast in pelvis when I got there, and dead - she did well - a boy.

9 Wife of Jason Sharp - Girl - both did well every way. Dec 10th 1858.

10 Negro of M. M. Weaver, all wright except that membrane adhered to womb, alittle fever - Slaughed off and did well Child girl March 20 1859.

11 Wife of D A Cook - Child Came with the Liquor amnii - had hard work to rupture membrane after head was born - all right Child boy March 28th 1859

12 Case Wife of Thos Litteral - all right Child boy - May 1st '59

13 Case Miss Angeline Maulden, Child born before I got there - It looked like foul play had been used - there were five holes in the occiput or crown of the head looked like it had been punched with some instrument - Child died - she lived, with hard work - perhaps had as well gone, however I can't say May 25 - 1859

14 Wife of Mr. Townsen - She had just
got over the flux, and was very weak
but by careful management she got through
well - all right - Child boy - June 28th

15 Black girl of Col. Ripley. She had no
difficulty in delivery - the placenta was
very tedious - child a boy. She did well - July 25th 1839

16 Wife of Thos. Morris - She commenced
flooding 8 days before hand - stopped it with
3 doses of nitrate of Potash - she lingered -
but finally got through well - all natural
child a boy. the 2 night she took three
very hard chills - extremities cold - put hot
rocks to feet - gave her a dose of Dover's
powders, & afterwards Castor oil - all over
in a short time - she did well from that
no more bad symptoms - July 30th 1839.

17 December 4. Wife of N. R. Roberts - all natural
- Child a girl.

18 Dec 13 Wife of James Akin - labor
natural - child a boy.

19 Dec 14 Black girl of A. J. Gill - Labor
natural - Placenta hard to remove
- did well - Child a girl.

20 case was my own wife - labor hard - presentation back of the neck - turned it by making pressure upwards in the absence of pain, before the waters came away - the head droped into the pelvis, and Labor terminated well child a boy - Jan. 3rd 1860 in the morning

21 case wife of Washington Jenkins - all right - Labor easy child a girl. Jan 5th '60

22 Servant of W Coleman - Placenta previa. very hard to manage - Considerable hemorhage Stopped with citrate of Potash - Both lived and did well - Child a boy. Jan. 21st 1860

23 Wife of Thos. Reves - all right in Birth but Placenta had adhered to womb. Child girl - February 26th '60

24 Wife of Dr. Vandiver, all right, Child very large - Boy - Born March 29th 1860

25 Wife of W. J. Haren - Labor lingering - but natural - Child a boy - Born April 4 - '60

26 Marion Fox wife - Labor natural - Child very large - a boy - April 17th 1860.

27 Wife of T. R. Weaver - womb closed in the morning at 8 - supposed it would be a slow labor - but little pain - left at 9 - came back 1/4 before 12 - child born & dead - had been for some days - child a boy - She did well - May 8th 1860

28 Wife of Samuel Barrett - labor [illegible]
tried nearly every thing to produce contraction of the
uterus - all failed - tried an enemata of Soap Suds
with 1 scruple Alois in it - uterine contraction
commenced - She was delivered of an unhealthy
Child - a boy - died next day. May 31st 1860

29 Wife of James P. Arrowood, premature - presenta
tion natis - Child dead - woman did well. - Boy -
June 5th 1860

30. Wife of Benjamine Parker, labor
very protracted - all right - placenta very
hard to remove - She did well child
a Girl June 8th 1860.

31 Wife of R. V. Blackstock - labor natural
all did well child a girl June 8th 1860

32 Wife of C. Barrett - first child
labor protracted - all natural - child
very large - tore the Perineum a
little nothing serious - all did
well - Child Girl

33 Wife of W. B. Cook she had been injured in a previous labor - did well this time - child a girl Aug. 9th '60

34 Girl negro of M. M. Weavers - slow labor had child to turn - all did well - she was taken with severe hemorrhage - gave her Laudanum Child a boy - Sept. 5th '60

35 Wife of W. B. Cheek - all right she did well - Child Boy - Nov. 5th '60

36 Wife of Wm Jenkins - presentation novel - had it to turn - child died a boy - she did well - Nov. 22 - '60

37 Wife of Wesley Eller - Birth natural Placenta adhered - removed by entering hand - woman Histerica did well - child girl - Dec. 16th '60

38 Wife of Samuel Wilson - Birth natural - first child - Boy Dec 21st 1860

39 Wife of Toly Hampton - natural Child a Boy Dec 26th 1860

40 Wife of Nathan Buckner - labor very protracted - nature not acting any - used Erg first child - All did well in the end Child a boy Jan 18th 1861

41 Wife of Rev. H. P. Waugh — Labor natural
all did pretty well — Child a girl — Jan 26th
42 Servant girl of M. M. Wiams's — labor
natural — Child boy — Feb 1st 1861
43 Wife of J. T. Weaver — labor natural
Child a girl — born Feb. 14th — 1861
44 Wife of Andrew Lankford — Womb
turned back — hard to keep otherwise — she
did well in the end — Girl — Feb. 17th '61
45 Wife of Rev. W. F. Parker — all
right — labor natural — Girl — Feb 27th '61
46 Wife of A. W. Ward — labor natural
Child a Boy — March 4th '61
47 Wife of James H. Ellis — Labor
Natural — Placenta adhered, and
had to be removed by force — she flooded
very severely — did well — Girl — March 10th
48 Wife of Thos. Litteral — Child cross
wise — turned and delivered — saved
both mother & child = Boy = March 17th
49 Wife of Henry A. Edwards — Had been in
labor 4 days before I went — Labor had
stopped — tried Ergot, vice versa, Sinapis,
to no effect. Steamed her with Brandy poured on
a hot rock — saved her — lost child — Girl
March 22nd '61

50 Lucinda Hyatt - She had the dropsy and was swelled all over - did well considering - she lived - child died next day. Child Boy - March 30th 1861

51 Wife of Robert J. Branch - all did well - Labor natural - child Girl April 1st '61

52 Wife of Kelsey Ray - Child born before I got there - Placenta attached - all right in a short time - Girl - April 15th 1861

53 Wife of Wm. M. Weaver - all natural Child a Girl. April 17th 1861

54 Wife of Elijah Chandler - Womb turned backwards - had to be held to its place labor tedious - mother & child did well - Girl April 24th 1861

55 Wife of John H Colfee - Labor natural, but very tedious child a Girl. June 22nd '61

56 Wife of W. C. Garrison - labor natural, except that the water gone way in the begining - first child very tedious - Child girl June 25th '61

57 Negro girl of W.K. Bairds child born when I got there - had been 7 hours - she unchained I cleaned her in 20 minutes all right. Child boy
[illegible]

58 Miss Frances Wilson - first
Child - Labor very rigorous - vomiting
very often - Child boy July 9th 61

59 Negro girl of W. H. B[illegible] - Labor
natural - did well - Child girl - July 19 61

60 Wife of Rev. M. W. Pickins - first
Child - Labor natural - Child Boy July 20

61 Wife of W. W. Jones - first child
all natural - did well - girl. Aug 14th

62 Wife of Charles McKinney -
first child. notes presented - [illegible]
labor - very difficult. - Boy -
dead when born Dec 5th 1861
She did well

63 Negro girl of Alex Munday
all right - Placenta fast - removed
it and all did well - Boy [illegible] Dec

64 Wife of James Akin - All
right - Child Girl. did well
Dec 20th 61

65 Wife of Jesse Barrett - all
right - She had received a scare
that day that had like to have caused
her death - finally did well
Child Boy Dec 27th 61

66 Lizza Surat – Child dead

67 Wife of H. P. Waugh – Labor natural did well for three days – took Puerperal Mania of the worst kind, and died the 11th day in the morning – the Child was a girl

68 Wife of James Sawyer Shoulder presentation – threw it back – head fell in pelvis, all did well. Child Boy. April 10th 62

69 Wife of W. H. Garrison When I got there she had been in labor 3 days – had been handled a great deal – was swelled – os uteri & labia &c so that inflammation was set up so that I could do nothing but subdue it – did so in one week – labor set in and she was delivered without help – child a boy, but dead. May 16th

70 Servant Girl of M. M. Mcanis All right – Did well every way. Child a mulatto girl – June 7th 1862

71 Wife of Thos. [illegible] - Had been
very feeble for some time but
the Labor was natural though not
hard - did well every way - Child girl

72 Mary Jane Buckner - all natural
Child a girl - July 16th '62

73 Wife of Wm Sterling - all right
Child a boy. July 19th 1862

74 My wife - Labor natural - child
a girl July 28th 1862

75 Wife of Joshua West, Labor
natural - Child a girl, all
did well - Aug. 8th '62

76 ~~76~~ Wife of Rev. J. S. Weaver
Labor natural - She did well - child
a girl - Sept. 10th 1862

77. Wife of Rev. Dr. Vandiver
Labor natural - all did well
child a Boy; Sept. 25th '62

78 Wife of A. M. Fox - He refused
to fight for the South, and took to
the mountains - left his wife to the
mercy of others - She did tolerably well
child a very large girl. Oct. 29th '62

79 Wife of Lafayette Frost - Her first child
He died at his brother A. M. - She
did well - all right - Child a
very large boy Nov. 12th '62

80 A Servant of Col. J. M. Sorrel.
She had lost 5 or 6 children in
child birth - they all had to be turned
I turned this one and saved it
Child a girl - Nov. 12th '62

81 Wife of Rev. Elias Jones - She
commenced flooding two days before
her child was born - had had
several miscarriages - Had been
threatened at the 6 & 7 month again
large clots passed each time I
gave her opium &c and stopped it
She went to her time - labor slow
but natural - She did well
Child a girl - Dec. 5th '62

82 Wife of J. H. Calfee - I let
her inhale Ether - She bore
a natural and safe delivery
child a girl - all did well
Dec 6th 62

83 Wife of Thos. Parker. Her husband is in the army. She did well - Child a girl Dec 10th '62

84 Wife of R.V. Blackstock. She did well - Labor natural but protracted - child a girl Dec 28th '62 -

85. Wife of Col. Reynolds - all did well - Labor natural - Child a girl.

86 Widow of Mr. Bradly - He died some two months ago. She had been in labor some 30 hours before I got there - On examination I was satisfied that it was a case of Hydrocephalis. I waited however some 24 hours as I had no chance of a consultation, and as I regarded her life in danger I performed Craniotomy, and then delivered her with forceps. She did tolerably well - Child a boy - Jan 20th '63

87 Wife of Rev. E. W. Moore. It was her first child. The water had broken before I got to her. The labor was natural in every way child a boy Feb. 15th '63

88 Wife of Willis Hughey. She was flooding very much when I got there — The child was born just as I entered the room. The Placenta was removed in about ½ hour, as it refused to come away — I stopped the flooding by giving Ergot — She did well
Child a Boy — March 6th '63

89 Wife of Rev. R.W. Pickens
Hemorrhage from the beginning gave her Ergot. All did well
Child a boy March 19th '63

90 Wife of Capt I.B. Nelson
Labor natural — all did well
Child a boy — March 26th '63

91 Negro girl of M.M. Means
Labor natural — all did well
Child a boy. April 4th '63

92 Wife of Madison Horn
all natural. all did well
Child a boy. April 8th '63

93 Wife of W.B. Cheek — all right
Child a girl — May 1st 1863

94 Wife of Maj. G. H. Britton
all natural — Child a girl
May 24th 1863

95 Wife of Charles McKinney
She was delivered of the Child
before I got there but the womb
Closed on the Placenta, I relieved
her in a short time — all did well
Child a boy — May 30th '63

96 Negro Girl of Mr. M. Weaver
all right — Labor natural
Child a boy. June 15th '63

97 Daughter of Mr. Bowen's wife — She
had deceived her mother, and the child
was born before I got there — I cleared her
She did well — Child a girl June 26th '63

100. Wife of William Clounty — Child
born before I got there — She did tolerably
well. Child girl — June 26th '63

101 Servant girl of J. S. Burnett — Hard labor
Did well Child a Girl — June 28th 1863

102 Wife of James Sawyer — Child born
before I got there — Did well —
child girl June 29th '63

103 Wife of Capt Parker - she had natural labor - Child a boy - did well - Sept 9 1863 -

104 Liza Sarat - Labor natural Child a girl - did well Sept. 28th

105 Wife of Wisby Ellen - labor natural all did well - Child girl - Nov 18th '63

106 Wife of W. C. Garrison - labor protracted and hard - did well Child Girl. Dec 1st '63

107 Wife of Rev. J D Baldwin, labor natural - did well - Child Boy, Dec 4th '63

108 Wife of A. D. Fair - she had been rather dropsical for some months - did well - labor natural - Child Boy Feb. 29th '64

109 Wife of J. H. Ellen - all right Child a Boy. March 7th '64

110 Girl of W R Baird - When I got there the Bladder was pushed down before the Child's head - put it back when the pain was of - She has Neuralgia of the womb hence suffers greatly - Stayed Dirt dobber's nest - decoction - it acted as strong as Ergot and resembles its action - Child very feeble a boy - March 10th '64

111 Servant Girl of J. T. Weaver – Labor natural – Child a girl March 11th '64

112 Wife of James Parker – Labor natural Feb 28th '64 Child Girl

113 Daughter of William Jump – first Child – Labor very hard & tedious Child large – Boy – both did well for 13 days – mother took fits, had 17 in 24 hours – Bled, cupped & purged – she recovered, Born March 15th '64

114 Wife of Wyatt Runnion – had been in labor 24 hours – Shoulder presentation – arm out of birth place – gave Morphine turned child and it was born – child dead – Girl. March 20th '64

115 Wife of Thos. Garrison, labor natural – Placenta adheared – had to enter hand and remove it – done with difficulty, both did pretty well child a Boy – March 19th '64

116 Wife of Marion Fox – all right Labor natural – Child Girl April 3rd 1864 –

117) Wife of Washington Tomkins - Labor natural
child a girl. July 15. 1864

118. Wife of Wm. M. Weaver - Labor natural
child a boy Aug. 22nd 1864.

119 Wife of John West jun. Labor hard but
natural. Child a girl Aug. 24. 1864

120 My wife - Labor natural child a boy
Nov. 7 at 12½ O'clock P.M.

121 Wife of Col. J. M. Ray - Labor natural - child
a boy. Dec. 11 - 1864

122 Wife of Rev. Wm Briggs - Six month
child - gave her Ergota - did well child died
It was a boy. Feb. 19. 1865

123 Wife of Montraville Black - Labor very hard,
all right. Child a boy 12th Feb 1865

124. Wife of Rev. R. M. Pickens - Labor natural
child a girl Feb 21st 1865

125 - Wife of Samuel Barrett. Labor natural
child a girl March 21st 1868

126 Wife of James Sawyer - all right
child a girl April 1st. 1865 -

127 Wife of Rev. J. S. Weaver. Labor natural
child a boy. April 15th 1865 -

128 Wife of J. M. Harris – Labor natural
child a girl. April 25th 1865

129 Wife of Thos. Rivis. Labor hard but
all right. Child a girl May 17. 1865

130. Wife of Cary Weaver – Bladder came
down in advance of the childs head – put it
back – did well – child girl – July 4th. 1865

131 Ben Weaver's wife – all right.
child a girl. July 8th 1865

132 Wife of Wm Sterling – Labor natural
child a boy. Aug. 17. 1865

133 Sam Weaver's daughter child a girl
labor natural. Sept 5. 1865

134 Wife of William Surrat – first
child – parts small – Hard labor, did
well – child a boy Oct. 8th '65

135 Wife of Mitchel Garrison – She
had fever, and was prematurely delivered – had to extract after birth – did
well under the circumstances – Oct. 14th '65

136 Wife of Wm Bowen – Labor
natural – child a boy. Nov. 12

137 Wife of Pinckney Buckner
Labor natural Child Boy. Nov. 26

140 Wife of Dr. Vanduim — Labor natural — used Ether — all did well — Child a boy — Dec. 13th '65

141 Wife of William Black — Labor natural — Jan 8 '66 Boy,

142 Miss Mary Wagoner — Womb turned back — Labor difficult — did well Child a boy Jan 20th 66

143 Wife of William Jones — Labor natural but slow — all right — Child Boy

144 Wife of Matt. Jones — Labor unusually hard — all right — child a boy.

145 Wife of Washington Jenkins — Labor natural — Child a Girl — She had afterwards Inflammation of the Labia — Jan 28

146 Wife of Robert Rutledge — Labor natural did well — Child a boy Jan. 30th 66.

147. Wife of J. H. Ellen — She commenced waisting 10 days before delivery — Child had to be turned — Placenta grown fast — She lived child died — Girl — Feb 10. '66.

148 Wife of J. H. Calpin — Labor protracted did well — child a Boy. Feb 11th 66

149 Wife of James Atkin — Labor natural did well — child a boy — Feb 12th '66

150 Mrs. Shockly - Labor natural
Child a boy, Feb. 16th 66 =

151 Negro girl Jinny, Labor natural
Child a boy - March 2nd '66

152 Wife of William Davis - Labor natural
child a girl - March 20th '66

153 Wife of J. P. Black - premature labor - caused
by debility - child a girl March 26th 1866.

154 Wife of James P Black - She was
in last stage of Consumption - premature labor - Child girl & died - she
lived two days March 26th 1866.

155 Wife of G. W. Genty - Labor natural
child a boy - both did well - March 30 -

156 Priscilla, a Negro girl - Labor
natural, Child a boy April 13th '66

157 Miss Ann McClellan - first child
labor hard but natural - child
a boy April 15. 1866.

158 Wife of G. W. Branch - labor
natural - child girl - May 17th '66

159 Wife of Alexander Wagoner - Labor
natural - Child a girl - May 20. '66

160 Wife of Wm Kigler. Labor natural
Child a girl. May 23d 1866

161 Wife of Wm Carey. Labor natural
Chil a girl. June 27th 1866

162 Wife of Cannady Ryman - first
Child - labor natural - did well
Child 8 months & a girl July 2nd

163 Wife of Col. Daniel Reynolds.
labor natural - Placenta hard to
remove - Child a girl July 6th

164. Wife of Wm. Spence - Labor natural
Both did well. Child a boy - July 28th 1866

165 Wife of Newton Gentry - first child -
Labor natural - Child a girl Aug. 15th 1866

166 Wife of M. R. Edmonds - Labor
very protracted - and difficult.
Did well - Child a girl. Aug 20th '66

167 Wife of R. V. Blackstock - labor
natural - Child a boy - Sept. 5th '66

168 This was a case of Dropsy of Amnion
Wife of Allen Edwards. The pressure was
so great on the vital organs that I had
to puncture the sack - drew off 6 gals water
brought on labor had 2 dead children, Both
boys - She did well - Sept. 13th '66

169 Wife of Joseph Chearley - Labor very hard - Feet presented
Child died - Girl - Sept. 12th 66
170 Wife of Elisha Clark - Labor natural
Child a girl - Sept. 26th 1866
171 Wife of Highy Hamilton - first labor - Natural - Child Girl - Sept 29 - '66
172 Wife of Dr. Harris - Labor natural
first child - a boy - Oct 23rd 66
173 Wife of W. Clinton - all right
did well - Child, Boy, Nov 7th '66
174 Wife of Elias Jones - all right.
did well - Child Boy - Nov 18th '66
175 Wife of Robt. Ramsey - first child
did well - Child Girl - Nov 10th '66
176 Wife of Thos. Parker - Labor
natural - Child girl - Dec 21, '66
177 Wife of D. Hunsucker - Labor
natural - Child Girl - Jan 9th '67
178 Wife of James Cole - Breast presentation - turned the child - threw its head in Pelvis - Labor natural - Child Boy - Jan 13th '67
179 Wife of Rev. R. H. Pickens - Labor natural - Child Boy - Jan 20th '67

180 Wife of Milton [illegible] - Labor natural child a Girl - May 13th 1867

181 Wife of Miles Coleman - Labor natural child Boy - June 2nd 1867

182 Wife of Wm. Mc Weaver - Labor natural child Boy - June 18th 1867

183 Wife of Joseph Kiger - labor natural - child a Girl June 22nd 1867

184 Wife of Joseph Grotz - Labor natural - except that the water broke at the commencement, and made it tedious - first child - Girl June 29 '67

185 Wife of Madison Horin - Labor natural - Child a girl July 16th '67

186 Wife of Montiaville Black - Labor natural - Child a girl - July 23rd '67

187 Wife of Wash Jenkins, natural labor child a Girl - Aug 12th 1867

188 Mrs. Myra Gentry - Labor natural - child a Girl - Aug. 15th 1867

189 Wife of Alexander White - labor at 8 months water broke 3 day before delivery - Labor hard. Child Small & a Girl - Aug 25th 1867.

190 Miss Rebecca Etter - Labor at 7 months - water broke 3 day before labor commenced - Delivered of a Girl child - 24 hours after of a boy, Aug 26th & 27

191 Wife of Joseph Chambers - Labor natural
child a girl weighed 12 lbs - did well Aug 29th 1867

192 Wife of Joseph Tharp jun - Labor natural
except water broke 3 days before labor set in - Child
a boy Sept. 2nd 1867

193 My own wife - Water broke 3 days before labor
set in. did well Child a girl Sept. 8th 1867

194 Wife of Henry Jenkins - Labor natural
child a boy. Sept. 11th 1867

195 Wife of William Brown - Labor natural
child a girl Sept. 18th 1867

196 Wife of Lemuel Weaver Labor natural
child a girl - Sept. 24th 1867.

197 Wife of James Davis - first child - labor
natural - Child a girl. Jan. 16th 1868

198 Wife of Thos Revis - labor natural
Child a girl - Jan 30th 1868.

199 Wife of Ben. Weaver - Labor natural
child a girl - Feb 9th 1868

200 Wife of Jo. Wallin - first child - labor
protracted - child a girl Feb 29th 1868

201 Mrs. Butler - Labor natural - Child a
Boy - March 4th 1868.

202 Wife of James Atkins Labor natural
Child a boy March 6th 1868.
203 Martha West - Bastard & negro at
that - labor natural - child a girl April 27th
204 Wife of Wilburn Ellen - labor protracted, but otherwise natural - child
dead born - a Boy. May 3rd 1868.
205 Wife of Wm Sterling - labor natural
the womb closed on the placenta, and
it was with difficulty that it could be
opened sufficiently to extract it.
Child a boy May 14th '68
206 Wife of Alexander Wagoner, labor
natural - Child a girl - May 22nd 1868.
207 Wife of James Sawyer, Labor natural
Child a boy June 11th 1868.
208 Wife of William Jenkins jun. Labor
natural - Child a girl June 11th '68.
209 Wife of John Robertson - first child
labor protracted - Child a girl June 16th '68.
210. Miss Polly Edmonds. Labor natural
Child a boy July 10th 1868.
211 Wife of Arnold Keith - Labor protracted
Child a Girl. July 12th 1868.

212 Wife of Mr Turner - Labor natural
Child a girl. July 13th 1868.

213 Wife of Henry Parker (Negro) Child
a boy. July 19th 1868

214 Miss Ellen (Negro) Labor protracted
Child a Boy. July 27th 1868.

215 Wife of Col. John A. Fagg - Labor natural
child a girl - did well - Aug. 4th. 1868.

216 Wife of Hughey Hamilton - Labor
natural - Child a girl Aug. 17th '68

217 Wife of Walker Bowen, first
Child - labor protracted - but natural
Child a boy Aug. 20th '68

218 Wife of William Spence - labor natural
Child a boy Aug. 22nd '68.

219 Wife of Chrisly Barrett - labor
natural - Child a girl Aug. 27th '68

220 Wife of Calm Munday - did well child
a boy. Sept 4th 1868.

221 Wife of James Edwards - labor natural -
first child - a girl - Sept. 4th 1868.

222 Wife of Robert Purland - primipara
labor protracted - did tolerably well
Oct 1st 1868

223 Wife of Rev. J. S. Moore - Primipara labor protracted - did well - child a Girl - Oct. 29 '68

224 Wife of J. McKinzler - Labor natural child a girl - Oct. 31st '68.

225 Wife of Joseph Chambers - Labor natural child a girl - Nov. 12 '68

226 Wife of S. H. Cooper - labor natural Child a girl Nov. 5th 1868,

227 Wife of Joseph Chambers - Labor natural - Child a girl Nov 13th 1868

228 Wife of Thos. Parker - Labor natural Child a girl - Dec. 3rd 1868

229 Wife of Dr Vandiver - Labor natural Child a girl Dec. 20th '68

230 [illegible] Littral - labor natural. Child a girl Jan 2nd 1869

231 Wife of Milton [illegible] - Labor natural child a girl - Jan. 5th 1869.

232 Wife of G. W. White - first child - labor protracted - Child a Boy. Jan 14th 1869

233 Wife of Samuel Wilson - Labor natural Child a Girl - Jan. 27th 1869.

234 Wife of Joseph Ayers - first child - Labor protracted - Child a Boy. Feb. 6th 1869

235 Wife of J. W. Garrison - first child - labor natural - Child a boy Feb. 12th 1869

236 Wife of J. R. Patterson - first child - Labor natural - Child a Boy - Feb. 13th '69

237 Wife of Thos. Draper - Labor natural, but protracted - Child Girl - Feb 17th '69

238 Wife of J. B. Weaver, first child - Labor natural, child a girl - Feb 19th 1869

239. Daughter of Mrs Jump - first child Illegitimate - labor natural - Child a boy. March 14

240 Wife of R. J. Branh. labor natural child a girl March 20 1869

241 Wife of Sam Roberts - first child. labor protracted - Child a boy - April 3rd 69

242 Wife of W. W. Jones. labor natural - Child a girl. April 12th '69

243 Black girl - name not known - labor natural child a girl - April 17th '69

244 Wife of R. V. Blackstock - labor natural child a girl. April 30th '69

245 Wife of James Keaton - Labor protracted - Placenta attached - Child a Boy. June 9th 1869

246 Wife of Rev. J. R. Ball. Labor natural
child a boy - June 12th '69
247 Wife of A. J. McAlpine - Labor protracted -
umbilical cord wound around the Sholder - child
died born - a fine Boy. June 25th '69
248 Wife of Sidney Woodson - labor protracted.
child a boy. July 3rd '69
249 Wife of Mitch Brawk - Labor
protracted - first child. Girl Aug 30 '69
250 Wife of Elisha Clark - Labor protracted
child a boy - did well - Oct 16th '69
251 Wife of John Hughs - labor natural
child a girl Oct 17th 1869
251 Wife of D. Hunsucker - Labor natural
12th child - Girl Oct 21st 1869
252 Wife of James Davis - labor natural
child a girl Oct 25th 1869
253 Wife of Whitehead - first child
all right - did well - "Boy" Dec 12th 1869
254 Wife of James Sawyer - presentation
back of Sholder - used evry effort to turn
and failed. Could get no Physician to con-
sult with - Child dead - hence I cut it away
Mother did well Dec 13th 1869 "Boy"

255 Wife of Rev. T. J. Rope - natural labor all did well - "Boy" Dec 14th 1869

256 Wife of Alex. Wagoner - natural labor all did well - Child "girl" Dec. 22nd 1869

257 Wife of Joseph Nizer - Labor protracted - all did well - Child "Boy" Dec 25th 1869

258 Wife of W. R. Edmonds - labor protracted Child a "boy" Jan 9th 1870

259 Wife of John Wright - first child - labor natural - Child a "girl" Jan 29th 1870

260 Wife of Wm M. Weaver - labor natural - Child a Boy, Feb. 8th 1870

261 Wife of William Ellis - Child born when I reached There - She was flooding very much - had to deliver after birth by force, She did well - Chid lived April 9th 1870

262 Wife of Wm Edmonds, sr. Labor natural - Child a boy June 26th 1870

263 Wife of Wm Lassiter - Labor protracted Child a girl July 7th 1870

264 Wife of Charles McKinney - breast presentation - Turned and delivered - Placenta attached - delivered it - Child dead, July 9th 1870

265 Wife of Mitchel Rymer. Labor protracted - Child a Boy July 19th 1870

266 Wife of Wm Ellis - first child - labor protracted - child a girl - July 27th 1870

267 Wife of Thomas Revis - Labor protracted Child a Boy - July 29th 1870

268 Wife of Wm Kigler - labor protracted child a girl Aug 1st 1870.

269 Wife of John Robertson - labor very severe - Nov. 18th 1870 - child a Boy

270 Wife of Sam Rymer. Labor natural - Child a Boy - Nov 25th 1870

271 Wife of Rev. J. S. Mann. Labor natural child a Girl - Nov. 28th 1870.

272 Wife of J. B. Mann - Child premature Labor protracted - Girl - Jan 19th 1871

273 Wife of Wm Davis. Labor natural Child a Girl - Jan 30th 1871

274 Wife of R. W. Pickens - Labor premature - child, Boy Jan 31st 1871

275 Wife of J. J. Mackey - Labor protracted Child a Boy. Feb 27th 1871

276 Wife of Hicks Barnard - labor natural child, Girl - April 1st 1871

277. Wife of [illegible] Williams - Labor protracted
child a Boy. April 14th 1871

278. Wife of Rev. E. H. Joiner - Labor natural
Child Girl. May 8th 1871.

279 Wife of Dennis Mist - Labor protracted
Child a Monstrosity - Head nearly like
a Bull dog in shape - Boy. May 16th 1871

280 Wife of Joel Brigisson - Labor natural
Child Girl - May 21st 1871

281 Wife of James Edwards - Labor protra-
-cted - child Boy - June 25th 1871

282 Wife of George White - Labor natural -
July 2nd 1871

283 Wife of Charles McKinney - Twins -
Both Boys - July 13th 1871

284 Wife of George Justice. Labor natural
Child a Boy - July 17th 1871

285 Miss Matilda Nelson. Labor protracted
child a girl July 20th 1871

286 Wife of Walker Griffin. Labor natural
child a Boy - July 25 1871

287 Wife of Isaiah Harm - Labor protracted
child dead - Boy - Aug 3rd 1871.

288 Wife of T. H. Mearn – Labor natural, Child Girl – Aug 4th 1871

289 Wife of J. M. Garrison – Labor severe child Girl – dead – Aug 11th 1871

290 Daughter of George Alexander – labor natural child Boy Aug 11th 1871

291 Wife of Jacob R. Roberts – labor natural Child a Boy. Aug 25th 1871

292. Wife of John Jenkins. labor protracted child Girl Aug. 30th 1871

293. Wife of James M. Garrison – labor very tedious – She had no liquor Amnii child dead – Sept 16th 1871

294 Wife of Thos. Garrison. Labor natural placenta attached – Child Girl. Sept 23rd '71

295 Wife of Elbert Roberts. Labor natural Child Boy Sept 25th 1871

296 Wife of J. Lee. Mearn. labor natural child Boy. Sept 26th 1871

298 Wife of Dr. Vandiver – labor natural Child Girl – Oct 20th 1871

297 Leah Blythe – natural – Girl – Oct 1st 1871

299 Wife of H. K. Rhea. Labor natural – Placenta attached – Child Boy. Oct 22nd 1871

300 Wife of J[illegible]
Child Boy. Oct 28th 1871.

301 Wife of Cudge Alexander — natural
child Girl — Nov. 18th 1871.

302 Wife of Chrisley Hughey — labor protracted — Child a Boy. Dec 8th 1871

303 Wife of Milas Thompson — labor
very complicated — Child girl Dec 7th '71

304 Wife of Lee Wright — labor protracted
child dead — Girl Dec. 9th 1871.

305 Wife of W. C. Ellen — Protracted & severe
child Boy. Dec. 10th 1871

306 Wife of Chrisley Kiger. labor natural
child Girl — Dec 11th 1871

307 Wife of A. J. McAlpine. labor natural
child Girl Dec 12th 1871

308 Wife of Hughey Hamilton — Natural
child Girl — Dec. 13th 1871.

309 Wife of Tilman Edmonds. natural
child Girl Dec. 25th 1871

310 Wife of Chrisley Rowland — protracted
child a Boy. Dec 25th 1871

311 Wife of Wm Roberts — Natural labor
child Boy. Dec 30th 1871

312 Wife of J. M. Garrison -
Labor, severe and protracted
Jan 19th - Child a girl.

313 Wife of W. C. Garrison - Womb thrown backwards - labor slow
Child Girl - Jan 22nd 1872

314 Wife of Rev. John Simmons
Labor natural - Child a Boy
Feb. 10th 1872

315 - Mrs. Lea - Labor natural
Child a girl Feb. 20th 1872

316 Wife of Elisha Clark, Labor natural
child a girl 22nd Feb. 1872

317 Wife of J. W. Kigler. Labor natural
Child a boy - March 5th 1872

318 Lum Huff - Labor protracted,
child a girl March 25. 1872

319 Wife of J. A. White. Labor protracted
Child a girl - April 16th 1872.

320 Wife of Joseph Kigen - Labor protracted
Child dead - Boy, May 1st 1872

321 Wife of W. E. Weaver - Labor natural
child a boy - May 10th 1872

322 - Wife of Jackson Holt. Labor natural
child a boy. June 4th 1872

323 Wife of Barnett [illegible] - natural labor
Child a girl - June 22d 1872

324 Wife of John McCabe - natural labor
Child a girl - June 26th 1872

325 Wife of George Alexander - labor natural
Child a boy - July 4th 1872

326 Ann Weaver - first labor - natural -
Child a girl. July 7th 1872

327 - Wife of Sid Woodson - labor protracted
Child a girl July 17th 1872

328 Wife of Dennis West - Child dead
labor severe - Boy - July 19th

329 Wife of Gordon. Labor natural
Child a girl July 20th 1872

330 Wife of George White - natural
Child a girl

331 Wife of T. M. Garrison first child
- natural - Boy. Aug. 28th 1872

332 Wife of Rev. T. M. Dula - Labor
natural - Child a boy - Sept. 8th

333 - Wife of Alf. Turner. natural
Child a boy - Sept. 12th - 1872

334 Josephine Smith - Labor protracted
Child a boy. Sept. 24th 1872

335 Wife of J. McGarrison - Boy 1873
336 Wife of Rev. J. D. Mears - Girl 1873
337 Wife of C. A. Nichols - Girl 1873
338 Wife of S. H. Mears - Girl 1873
339 Wife of J. L. Mears - Boy 1873
340 Wife of Wilkin Eller - Dead - 1873
341 Wife of Newt Guty - Boy - May 1st 1873
342 Wife of Hugh Hamilton - Girl
natural - Aug 3rd 1873
343 Wife of Freeman Weil - Boy. June 17th 1873
Labor natural
344 Wife of L. A. Keegan - natural - Girl
Aug. 14th 1873
345 Wife of Rev. H. C. Jones - Girl
Aug. 17th 1873.
346. Wife of Lee Weston - Girl -
Sept 11th 1873.
347. Wife of Dr. J. F. Harris - Girl
Sept. 24th 1873.
348. Wife of Mr. Barnard - Girl
Oct. 8th 1873.
349 Wife of James Sawyer - Boy
natural - Nov. 9th 1873.

[illegible] Wife of [illegible]
Nov. 30th 1873.

350 - Wife of Miles Thompson - Girl
natural - Dec. 3rd 1873.

351 Wife of Erving Ray - Boy.
natural - Feb. 8th 1874

352 Wife of R. P. Brittain - Girl
1st child - Feb. 22nd 1874

353 - Wife of Sam Hoff - Labor complicated
child - Boy. Feb. 25th 1874

354. Samuel Kerr's wife. Girl - March 6th '74

355 Wife of James Hembree -
natural. Boy. March 8th '74.

356 Wife of Samson Weaver - Colored - first
child tedious - Girl. March 31st '74

357 Wife of Wm Black - Boy - April 1st '74

358 Wife of James Black - Boy.

359 Wife of M. J. Clinton - first child
natural - Girl - April 3rd 1874

360 Wife of J. R. Sams - Labor natural
child a boy - April 11th 1874

361 Wife of J. M. Garrison - labor natural
child a girl - April 18th 1874

362 - Wife of James Spruill - Labor premature - Child dead - April 18th 1874

363. Wife of J. J. Wolf - Labor natural Child a boy - April 25th 1874

364. Wife of Penix - first child - labor protracted - Child Boy [illegible] 24th 1874

365 Wife of Sim. Edwards - Labor natural child a boy - June 30th 1874

366. Vol. Edward's wife - labor protracted Placenta attached July 6th 1874

367. Wife of John Ward - Labor protracted Child a girl - July 19th 1874

368. Wife of Dr. H. B. Moore - labor natural Child a girl - July 27th 1874.

369. Wife of Alfred Turner - labor natural Child a boy. Aug. 14th 1874

370. Wife of John Henderson - labor protracted Child a girl - Aug 25th 1874

371 Wife of Joshua Gibbs - Labor protracted - Placenta attached - Aug. 26

372 - Wife of W. A. Baird - labor natural child Girl Sept 1st 1874

373 Wife of W. C. Garrison - Labor protracted child Girl Sept. 1st 1874

374 - Wife of James Garrison -
Labor protracted - Child a girl - Nov 8 - 74
375 Wife of George White - Labor natural
Child a girl Nov. 26th 74
376 Wife of S. H. Mcann - Labor natural
Child a girl - Nov 30th 74
377 Wife of James Garrison - Labor
protracted - Child a Boy - Dec 25th 74
378 Wife of J. L. Mcann - Labor natural
Child a Boy. Feb 16th 1875
379 - Wife of H. Hooker - Labor severe
Child a Boy - April 16th 1875
380 Wife of Charlie Sorrells - Labor
natural - Child a Boy. May 23rd 75
381 Wife of Marshal Fox - Labor natural
Child a Girl. June 4th 1875
382 Wife of W. E. Weaver - Labor natural
Child a Boy. June 16th 1875
383 Wife of C. A. Nichols. Labor natural
Child a girl July 12th 1875
384 Wife of Frank Roberts - first
child - labor natural -
child a girl: Aug. 8th 1875

385 Wife of Sydney Woodson
Labor difficult - child Girl - Aug. 9th '75
386. Wife of J. A. Keith - first child
Labor natural - Girl - Aug. 18th '75 -
387. Wife of Dr. E. Baird - first child
Breach presentation - did well - Child Boy
Aug. 24th 1875 -
388. Wife of John Robeson - labor protracted
Child Girl - Aug. 30th 1875 -
389. Nancy Roberts - first child - Boy -
Natural labor - Sept. 19th 1875 -
390 Wife of Lee Penland - Boy
natural - Jan 7th 1876
391 Wife of Jacob Sams - Labor severe
Child died - Boy. Feb. 9th 1876
392 Wife of Burton Penland. She was
taken with Spasms - knew nothing -
delivered her with forceps - child
lived several days - Boy - Feb. 7th '76
393. Wife of E. Byrdy - Natural - Girl -
did well - Feb. 26th '76
394. Wife of Samuel Brank - natural
Labor did well - Child a Girl
March 26th 1876

395 Wife of G. W. [illegible] — Labor natural — Girl
did well — April 8th 1876

396 Wife of James Pearce. Labor natural — did
well — Child a Boy — April 22nd 1876

397 Wife of John Jones. Labor natural — Girl
did well — May 19th 1876

398 Daughter of J. M. Patton — Child crossways the
pelvis — used instruments — child dead
she did well. Boy. May 20th 1876

399 Wife of R. P. Brittain — did well
child a Boy July 2nd 1876

400. Wife of Matt. Edwards — Labor difficult
Child a Boy. ~~July~~ 5th 1876

401. Wife of D. N. Reagan — natural — Girl
Aug. 4th 1876

402 Wife of Joseph Cole — natural — Boy.
Aug. 4th 1876

403 James Hinely — child 8 months — very
small — lived — did well. Boy. Aug. 8th 1876

404 John Henderson's wife — labor protracted —
child a girl — Aug. 18th 1876

405 Wife of T. H. Weaver — natural — Girl
Aug. 18th 1876

406 Wife of J. R. Sams - Natural - Boy.
Did well - Aug. 19th 1876
407 Wife of Ashbell Carter - first child
did well. Boy - Aug. 25th 1876
408 Wife of H. C. Blackstocks - Boy.
Sept. 1st 1876
409. Wife of James Sawyer - child dead
hard labor. Girl - Sept. 2nd 1876
410 Wife of A. S. Weaver - Boy.
Sept. 28th 1876
411 Wife of Wisly Gill - natural
- Girl - Sept. 28th 1876
412 Wife of Milas Thompson - Labor
protracted - Turned the child - both did
well. Girl - Sept. 29th 1876.
413. Wife of Wm Ray - Labor severe
child dead - Boy. Nov. 5th 1876
414. Wife of W. C. Garrison - labor severe
child Girl - Nov. 20th 1876
415 - Wife of James Garrison - labor
natural - Girl - Nov. 29th 1876
416 Wife of John Wilson - Natural
Labor - Child a girl - Dec. 4th 1875

417 Wife of Thos. Howe - Labor natural - Child
a Girl - Dec. 22nd 1876

418 Wife of Levi Huff. Labor protracted
child a Boy - Jan. 23rd 1877

419 Wife of Wily Ramsey - Labor had
been on hands 3 days before I got there
she did well - Child a Girl Jan 25th '77

420 Wife of Lawson Weaver - labor
natural - Child a Girl - Jan 26th 1877

421 Wife of J. L. Weaver - Natural
child a Boy Feb 13th 1877

422 Wife of Alf. Lerner, Labor
natural - child Girl - April 6th '77

423 Wife of Milton Renn - child
cross - arm presentation - had to
turn and deliver April 18th 1877

424 Wife of George Hampton - first
child - Labor natural, but protracted
child a Boy - May 3rd 1877

425 Jane Elkins - Twins - Bastards
a Girl & a boy May 7th 1877

426 May 11th Wife of Frank Roberts
Labor natural - child a Boy.

427 Wife of W. K. Rhea - Labor premature
Child dead - Girl - June 24th 1877
428 Wife of Lee Henry - Natural labor -
Child Boy - July 16th 1877.
429 Wife of Dr. H. B. Weaver - Natural
Child a Girl - Aug. 22nd 1877
430 - Wife of Moore Ray - labor protracted
Child a Boy - Aug. 23rd 1877
431 Wife of Rev. W. F. Parker - labor natural
- Child a girl. Sept. 6th 1877
432 Wife of C. A. Nichols. Labor natural
Child a boy. Sept. 9th 1877
433. Wife of Marshall Williams. first child
labor natural - Child Boy - Sept. 10th 1877.
434. Wife of J. H. Robeson - first child.
labor natural. Child Girl. Sept. 12th 1877
435. ~~Wife~~ of James Black - first child
labor severe - Child Cross the pelvis -
Girl - Sept. 12th 1877
436. Wife of Dr. E. Baird - premature
labor natural - Boy - Sept. 17th 1877
437. Wife of Rev. A. J. Frazier, Labor
natural - Child Boy. Sept. 21st 1877

438. Wife of Capt. W. C. M[illegible] - labor [illegible]
Child a Girl Oct. 3rd 1877

439. Wife of S. M. Garrison - labor natural
child, Boy Dec. 4th 1877

440. Wife of John English - She had been injured - did well under the circumstances
Child a girl - Dec. 24th 1877

441. Wife of W. B. Smith - Labor natural -
child a boy. Jan. 8th 1878

442. Wife of Marshall Fair - first child -
labor natural - Jan. 16th 1878.

443. Wife of R. H. Weaver - labor protracted
Child a boy first child Jan. 27th 1878

444 Wife of Dr. Willis. Labor protracted
first Child - A Boy - Feb. 2nd '78

445 Wife of John Robeson - Labor natural
Child a Boy - Feb. 20th '78

446 Wife of Col. A. Baird. Labor natural
Child a Girl - Feb. 22d 1878

447 - Wife of E. M. Goolsby - first child
labor natural - Girl - Feb. 26th 78

448 - Wife of William Ray - labor natural
Child a Girl - Feb. 27th 1878

449 - Wife of Mr Roberts - first child labor natural - Boy - Feb. 27th 1878 -

450 - Wife of Mr Corbit - first labor - natural - Boy - March 7th 1878

451 - Wife of Alford Shepherd - first child - natural labor - Girl - March 19th

452 Wife of Robert Barrett - first child labor natural - Girl - March 26th 1878

453 Wife of Rev. Frank Pender - natural labor Placenta firmly attached - Girl - April 1st

454 - Wife of J. H. Mcann - natural labor Boy - April 12th 1878

455 Wife of Linnis West - labor natural child a Girl - April 16th '78

456 - Wife of James Pearce - natural labor Child a Boy - April 28th

457 Wife of Judson Haren - natural labor child a boy - June 18th 1878.

458 Wife of John Jones. Labor [illegible] child a Girl - July 17th 1878

459 Wife of Elias Sprouse - Labor natural child a Boy - Aug. 1st 1878

460 - Wife of George Peak - natural labor. Child Girl - Aug. 2nd 1878

461 Wife of William Clark Jr. [illegible] Labor & [illegible]
child a Girl – Aug. 7th 1878

462 Wife of Robert Buckner – Labor natural
child a Boy. Aug. 7th 1878.

463. Wife of Jackson Peak – Labor protracted
child a Girl – Aug. 13th 1878.

464 Wife of John Henderson – natural labor
child a Boy – Sept. 21st 1878

465 Wife of F. H. Tillinghast – Deaf & dumb
mother & father – also his wife – child Offspring
Girl – Sept. 22nd 1878

466 Wife of R. P. Brittain – natural labor
child Boy – Sept 24th 1878

467 Wife of James Joyner – natural
child a Boy. Sept. 27th 1878

468. Wife of Jesse Gwaltney – natural
child a Boy. Oct. 12th 1878

469 Wife of Joseph Moore – first child
natural – Girl Oct. 20th 1878.

470 Wife of Dr. E. Baird – natural
child a Girl Oct. 16th 1878

471 Wife of Robt. Flack – first child
Boy Nov. 15th 1878

472 Cora Tate - Colored - first child
Girl Nov 25th 1878

473 Jennie Brittain - labor protracted
Child Girl - Nov. 27th 1878

474. Wife of Arnold Keith - Labor protracted
child a girl Dec. 2nd 1878

475 Wife of Rev. S. S. Weatherly - first child
labor natural - child Boy - Dec. 3rd '78

476 Wife of W. D. Black - labor protracted
Child Girl Jan. 8th 1879

477 Wife of Dr. R. C. Brown - first child
labor natural - Child Girl Jan 23rd '79

478. Wife of W. A. Baird - natural labor
child a Boy Jan 24th 1879

479 Wife of A. S. Weaver -
child Boy Jan. 26th 1879

480 Wife of Jack Hunter
child Boy. Feb. 4th 1879

481 Wife of Henry Joiner - first child
Twins - Girl & a Boy Feb. 21st 1879

482. Wife of Arthur Shurrat - first
Child - natural - Boy. March 13th

483 - Wife of Wesley Gill - natural -
Girl. April 1st 1879

484 Wife of James Numbers natural Girl April 5th 1879.

485 Wife of Frank Ponder - labor natural - Placenta attached. Child a Boy - April 8th 1879

485 - Wife of R. N. Elkins - first child - did well March 16th 1879

486 - Wife of Isaac Coleman natural Boy - April 19th '79

487 - Wife of Charles Lovells - Child Cross wise - Elbo presenting turned - did well - April 23rd '79 "Girl"

488 - Wife of J. W. Roberts - Back presenting - turned - did well Child "Girl". April 9th '79

489 Wife of Robt. N. Weaver - natural - Child Girl - May

490 Wife of J. F. Paris - natural Boy - May 25 - 1879

491 Wife of A. H. Baird - Back presentation - turned child - Mother & child both did well - Girl - June 6th 1879

492 Wife of Ashbell Carter - Labor natural Girl - June 18th 1879

493 Wife of D. N. Reagan - Labor natural
child a Boy - July 5th 1879

494 Wife of Aneiva Howard - natural labor
Child Girl - Aug. 8th, 1879

495 Wife of Thos. Edwards - natural labor
Child Girl - Aug. 9th 1879

496 Wife of Henry Parker - Colored - natural
labor - Girl - Aug. 22nd 1879

497. Wife of Berry McAbee - Protracted labor
child Girl - Sept. 12th 1879

498 Wife of Lee Huff - Labor complicated.
Child Boy - Sept. 26th 1879.

499 Wife of H. P. Roberts - natural labor
child a Boy. Sept. 29th 1879

500. Wife of Dr. N. B. Weaver - natural labor
child Girl - Oct. 3rd 1879

501. Wife of L. M. Garrison - Premature
dead - Jan. 3rd 1880

502 Wife of M. Riddle - natural labor
child Girl - Jan 26th 1880

503 - Wife of W. E. Weaver - womb turned
far back - Boy - Jan 30th 1880

504. Wife of John A. Nichols - first child
Labor natural - Child Girl - Jan. 31st 80

505 Wife of C. A. Nichols - natural labor
child a boy. Feb. 17th 1880.
506 Wife of Dr. W. L. Ringam - first child
protracted labor - Boy - Feb 25th '80
507 Wife of Hy Sterling - first child - Protracted labor - Child Boy - March 9th '80
508 Wife of J. L. Weaver - Natural labor
Child Girl March 25th 1880
509 Wife of Dennis West. Labor natural
Child, Girl. March 30th 1880.
510 Wife of Rol. Flack - natural labor
child Boy - April 4th 1880.
511 Wife of T. H. Weaver - natural labor
Child Boy April 15th 1880.
512. Wife of Wm Edwards - labor premature - Placenta Previa - Girl - April 19th
513 Wife of A. S. Weaver - natural labor
child a boy May 4th 1880
514 Wife of Logan Mackey - first child -
labor natural - May 4th 1880. - Girl
515. Wife of Joseph Moore = natural labor
child Boy May 5th 1880.
516. Wife of Wiley Farnsworth - Colord -
Labor protracted - child a boy June 5th 1880

517 Wife of Milas Thompson - labor
protracted - Child a girl. June 5th '80
518. Wife of John Wilson - natural
labor - Child a Boy. June 18th '80
519 Wife of Bruce Flack - first labor
protracted - did well June 29th - Girl.
520 Wife of Miles Burgan - natural
labor - Girl - July 4th 1880.
521 Wife of Gilbert Elkins - did well
- Child Boy, July 5th 1880.
522 Wife of W. C. Garrison
- Child a Girl - July 5th 1880
523 Wife of John Henderson
Child a girl - July 19th 1880.
524 Wife of Bob Barrett - Child
cross ways - Turned, delivered
woman did well child dead
Oct. 12th 1880, ~~Girl~~ Boy
525 Wife of W. A. Baird - natural
Child Boy Nov. 5th 1880,
526 Wife of Elias Sprouse -
natural - Child Boy Nov 14th '80
527 Wife of Jacob Barrett - natural
Girl ~~Nov~~ 11th '80

528 Wife of W. H. [illegible] [illegible]
Dec. 8th 1880 [illegible])

529 Clora Tott - Colored - Boy - Dec. 12th '80

530 Wife of Dr. J. A. Harris - natural - child
Boy, Dec. 17th 1880

531 Wife of Thos. J. Farmer - first child -
Boy Dec. 22nd 1880.

532 Wife of Wm Calloway - natural
Child a Boy. Dec. 23rd 1880.

533 Wife of Wesley Roberts - first child
natural - Girl - Jan 3rd 1881

534 Wife of R. H. Mann - natural.
child Girl - Jan. 6th 1881

535 Wife of Thos. Guthrie - natural
child girl Jan. 10th 1881

536. Wife of James Whitehead - natural
Child Boy. Jan 13th 1881.

537 Wife of John Redden - natural
placenta adhered - child Girl. Jan. 22. '81

538 Wife of John Byram. natural
child Boy. Jan 24th '81

539 Wife of J. M. Garrison - Labor protracted
child a Boy. Jan 31st 1881.

540 Wife of James Jones - natural
child Girl - Feb. 11th '81
541 Wife of J. F. Barris - natural
child Boy, Feb. 12th 1881.
542 Wife of R. P. Brittain - premature
child dead - Boy Feb 28th '81
543 Wife of John Parris - natural
child Boy. Feb. 28th '81
544. Wife of Douglas Weaver, first
child - Girl - March 7th '81
545. Wife of John Hughs. Placenta
Previa. Two children - Boy &
Girl - Died of Hemorrhage. March 29
546 Wife of Marshall Williams
child Girl April 11th '81
547. Wife of Rev. J. C. Cannon
child. Girl. April. 13th '81
548 Wife of Matt. Black
child Boy. April 23rd '81
549. Wife of James Hampton
first, Girl - April 24th '81
550 Wife of Albert Ellen - natural
child a Girl - May 20th '81

551 Wife of Bill Pickens (Colored) / nat.
Child - Girl - May 24th 1881

552. Wife of J. A. Gwaltney - natural
Child Girl - June 6th 1881

553 Wife of Mc Cook - Labor protract-
-ed - Child Boy - June 11th 1881

554 Wife of Wm. M. Davis - natural
Child Girl - June 15 - 1881

555 Wife of Jacob Willis - delivered
with forceps - child and mother
both did well. July 3rd 1881 - Girl

556 Wife of Wm Bowen - natural
Child Girl - July 4th 1881

557 Wife of James Cook - natural
Child Girl - July 22nd 1881

558 Wife of Newton Cook - natural
Boy - July 30th 1881

559 Wife of Berry McCabe - natural
Child - Boy - Aug. 3rd 1881

560 - Wife of Joseph Moore - natural
Boy - Aug 5th 1881

561 - Wife of Thos. Tillinghast - natural
Boy. Aug Aug. 24th '81

562 - Wife of Jimmy Pauland - tedious
Boy Aug 26th '81

563 Wife of James Reace - labor natural - Child Girl - Sept. 18th 1881

564 Wife of Wesly Gill - natural labor Child Boy - Sept 19th - 1881

565 Wife of F. P. Roberts - labor natural Child Boy - Oct. 2nd 1881

566 Wife of Joe Philips - Fallopian conception - child had been 4 months decended through tube - born through vagina - woman did well.

567 Wife of Jack Hunter - natural labor - Child Girl. Nov. 4th 1881

568 Wife of Rev. Amos Justice - natural labor - Child girl. Dec 26th 1881

569 Wife of J. H. Weaver - natural labor. Child Boy - Jan 20th 1882

570 Wife of Henry McCabe - protracted labor Child Girl - Jan 21st 1882

571 Wife of Thos. Edwards - protracted labor child boy - Jan. 27th 1882

572 Wife of Robt. P. Brittain - protracted labor. - child Girl - Feb. 21st 1882

573 Wife of John Hudleson - Twins both Girls - Feb. 23rd 1882

574 - Wife of Rev. John [illegible] - [illegible]
labor natural - child Boy March [illegible]

575 - Wife of J. L. Mann - natural
child Boy March 7th 1882.

576. Wife of W. H. Hunter - natural
child Boy March 9th 1882

577 Wife of James Keith - protracted
child Boy March 17th 1882

578 Wife of Roll Flack - natural
child Boy March 18th 1882

579. Wife of George W. Bell - protracted
child Boy. March 18th 1882

580 Wife of Bruce Flack - natural
child Boy - March 19th 1882

581 Wife of Bob Morehead - natural
child Girl - April 3rd 1882

582. Wife of Spivy - natural
child Boy April 11th 1882.

583 - Wife of [illegible] Frost - Premature
- 6 months - Boy. April 12th 1882

584 - Wife of A. Howard - Labor natural
child Boy. April 20th 1882

585 Wife of Rev. J. P. Allen - first child
Wife 48 years old - Girl - dead - mother did well. May 4th

586 - Wife of Logan Mackey - Did well
Child Boy, May 5th 1882
587 Jennie Brittain - Did well.
Boy, May 6th 1882
588 Wife of Col. Baird - Did well
child Boy, May 7th 1882
589 Wife of Wesly Roberts - Did well
child dead - Boy - May 12th 1882
590 Wife of Jacob Chambers - Did
well - Child Boy - May 13th 1882
591 Wife of Wm. Black Did well
child Boy. May 24th 1882
592 Wife of T. M. Garrison - Did well
child Girl - May 27th 1882
593 Wife of Arthur Pegram - Did
well - Child Girl June 1st 1882
594 - Wife of Joseph Gentry - Natural
child "Girl" - June 11th 1882
595 Wife of M. Lovelace - natural
Boy - June 24th 1882
596 Wife of McBurgan - natural
child Boy - June 25th 1882
597 Wife Thos. Tate - Spasms, before
and after birth Boy, June 27th '82

598 Wife of Robt White natural
Child "Boy" July 3rd 1882

599 Wife of Robt Black – breast presentation
turned and delivered Boy – July 10th

600 Wife of J. R. Sams – natural labor
child Girl July 17th 1882

601 Wife of W. B. Smith – labor natural
child Boy – July 22nd 1882

602 Wife of Ramsey – labor protracted
Dr. Craigmiles case – he had the os
to cut in 4 places – child cut away – woman
did well – child boy – July 27th 1882

603 Wife of J. M. Cooley – natural labor
child Girl – Aug 13th 1882

604 Wife of Miles Thompson – labor
natural – protracted – Girl Aug 14th '82

605 Wife of Alfred Newton – natural
child Girl – Aug. 22nd 1882

606 Wife of Isaac Coleman – natural
child Boy Aug. 25th 1882

607 Wife Sam Tate – primipara – natural
child girl – Sept 24th 1882

608 Wife of James Simer – natural
child Boy October 2nd 1882

609 wife of Joseph Chandler - head in
front of pubis - otherwise natural
child a Girl - Oct. 13th 1882

610 wife of Wm Parrish jr. - natural
child a girl - Oct. 14th 1882

611 wife of Charles Lawson; primaparia
had to use instruments - both did
well - Girl - Oct. 23rd 1882

612 wife of George Peak - natural -
except cord knotted - Girl - Oct. 28. 1882

613 wife of W. McRobertson - first child -
did well - Boy Nov. 10 - 1882

614 wife of James Hamblin - did well
natural labor - Girl - Nov. 12th 1882

615 wife of H. C. Blackstocks - natural
child a Boy (Girl) Nov 16th 1882

616 wife of W. O. Conner - first child
natural - Boy - Nov. 20th 1882

617 wife of J. A. Gwaltney - natural
child Boy - Nov. 25th. 1882

618 wife of Elias Sprouse - natural
labor - child Girl Dec 7th 1882

619 wife of R. H. Mcann - natural
child a Girl - Dec. 12th 1882

620 Wife of Harry Shields - natural labor - Child girl Dec 21st 1882

621 Wife of John Parris - labor protracted - Child a Boy Dec 22nd 1882

622 Wife of George Rudd - first child natural labor Child Girl - Dec. 28th 1882

623 Wife of Marion Martin - first child protracted - Child Boy - Jan 2nd 83

624 Wife of Benj. Brucie - natural labor - Child Girl - Jan 4th 1883

625 Wife of Douglas Mearn - natural labor - Child a Boy - Jan 11th '83

626 Wife of T. S. Morrison - natural labor protracted Feb 9th Boy. '83

627 Wife of W. A. Baird - labor protracted Child a Girl - Feb 17th '83

628 Wife of James B. Mearin - first child natural labor - Boy - March 12th '83

629 Wife of Daniel Taylor - first child natural labor - Girl - March 14th '83

630 Wife of J. Crook - natural Child a Girl - March 23rd '83

631 Wife of J. J. Riagan - first labor protracted - Child girl - April 8th '83

632 Wife of J. H. Mearn - She had measles badly at her confinement, but did well - Child lived 10 days. Boy. April 10th

633 Wife of A. Howard - labor premature. She did well - Boy - May 1st 1883.

634 Wife of James Whitehead - natural labor - Child Boy, May 5th 1883

635 Wife of C. A. Nichols - She fell 8 feet 2 months before time - Labor began - Hemorrhage set in - I stopped both with Black Haw Tea & Morphia - she went to time did well - Child girl. May 24th '83

636 Daughter of Albert Martin - first child - did well - Girl - May 31st 1883

638 Wife of Matt Black - natural Boy - Aug 3rd 1883

637 Wife of Harry Wright - first child natural - Boy - July 31st 1883

639 Wife of Bob Crago - natural Child - Boy - Aug 23rd 1883

640 Sis Rush, alias, McIntyre natural - Child Girl. Sept. 12th 1883

641 Wife of Wm Hamilton - natural labor - Child girl - Sept. 18th 1883

642 Wife of M. B. Smith – Twins [illegible]
both doing well. Children Girls – Sept 2[illegible] 1883

643 Wife of Thos. L. Weaver – first child – did well – Girl – Sept 28th 1883

644. Wife of Milton Keever – natural labor Boy – Oct. 16th 1883

645 Wife of Wesley Roberts – natural Child Girl Dec 12th 1883

646 Wife of Marshal Fain – natural Child Boy – Dec – 25th 1883

647 Wife of John Davis – natural child a girl Jan 10th 1884

648 Wife of J. A. Gwaltney – natural Child Boy Jan 11th 1884

649 Wife of Mathias Smith – natural Child Girl ~~Jan~~ 15th 1884

650 Wife of Albert Ellis – natural Child girl Jan 15 – 1884

651 Wife of Chris Fox – Contracted Pelvis – Craniotomy – Boy Jan 17

652 Wife of J. L. Weaver – Premature labor Child Girl Jan 21st 1884

653 Wife of M. W. Robertson – natural Child Boy – Jan. 22d 1884

654 Wife of Charles Hom—
natural - Child Boy Jan. 22nd '84

655 Wife of Roll Flack - natural
child Boy Jan 23rd 1884

656 Girl at Thos. Shufords - negro -
natural - Girl Jan 31 - 1884

657 Wife of Rev. Cain Atkins - natural
child Girl - Feb 22nd 1884

658 Wife of Alex Cain - first child
natural - Girl - March 17th '84

659 Wife of Thos. Edwards - natural
child Boy March 26th 1884

660 Wife of John Lovelace - natural
child Boy April 16th 1884

661 Wife of Dennis West - Premature
deformed - Boy April 23rd 1884

662 Wife of ~~John~~ Wilson - natural
- Boy April 24th 1884

663 Wife of Rev. W. P. Deane - natural
child Girl April 27th 1884

664 Wife of A. S. Weaver - natural
child Boy - May 1st 1884

665 Wife of Calvin Shepherd - child dead
Boy - Instrumental delivery - She lived
May 14th 1884

666 Wife of J. C. Weaver - natural child girl - June 1st 1884.
667 Wife of John Henderson - natural child Girl - June 15th 1884
668 Wife of W. A. Baird - natural child girl Sept. 9th 1884
669 Wife of Rufus Weaver - natural child girl - Sept. 9th 1884
670 Wife of James Jenner - natural child girl - Sept. 10th 1884
671 Wife of Sam Hoff - labor tedious child a girl Dec. 9th 1884
672 Wife of Wesley Gill - natural child a Boy Dec 18th 1884
673 Wife of N. C. Blackstocks - natural child girl Dec. 27th 1884
674 Wife of Sam Johnson - child had been dead 2 months - decaying Jan 21st 1885
675 Wife of R. H. Weaver - natural child girl - Feb. 25th 1885
676 Wife of Joseph Calloway - natural child a Boy - March 13th 1885
677 Wife of Shipley Parker - first child Girl - March 10th 1885

678 Wife of John Davis - natural
child Girl March 1st 1885

679 Wife of Shisly Pendland natural
child Boy April 14th 1885

680 Wife of Dr. W. J. Clontz - Natural
both did well - Girl April 28th 1885

681 Wife of James Peeler
natural child Girl May 6th '85

682 Wife of James Black - child
cross wise - dead - woman did well
Girl May 9th 1885

683 Wife of Dennis West - natural
child a boy - May 12th 1885

684 Wife of Thos L. Mearns - natural
child Boy - May 27th 1885

685 Wife of Thos Davis - natural
child Girl June 3rd 1885

686 Wife of Will Pickens - natural
Child Boy - June 20

687 Wife of McFain - first child
Boy - natural - July 24th 1885

688 Wife of Matt. Black, child cross
ways - Girl - Aug. 4th 1885

689 Wife of J. S. [illegible]
Boy – natural labor Sept 3rd 1885
690 Wife of W. C. Sams – first child.
natural labor – child girl Sept. 14th 85
691 Wife of Joseph Chambers – child
girl – Oct 11th 1885 –
692 Wife of James Whitehead.
child girl. Nov. 5th 1885 –
693 Wife of Charles Hanson – natural
"Boy" Dec. 24th 1885 –
694 Wife of Joseph Ranham – natural
"Boy" Dec. 25th 1885 –
695 – Wife of Albert Ellen – protracted
"Boy" Jan 2nd 1886.
696 Wife of Rolla Flack – natural
"Girl" Jan 2nd 1886
697 Wife of James Penland –
protracted – Girl – Jan. 25th 1886
698 Wife of C. P. Weaver – first child
natural – Peritoneum ruptured – Boy Feb.
699. Wife of Wm Kirkendall – protracted
child died – "Boy". Feb 5th 1886
700 – Wife of Jef. Donnahoo – first
child natural Boy. Feb 25th 1886

701. Wife of Lee Hey - natural labor
Child a boy - Feb. 27th 1886

702 Wife of Thos. Edwards - natural
Child Boy - March 11th 1886

703. Wife of John Henderson -
natural - Chil Boy. March 14th 1886

704 Wife Ed. Byerly - natural -
Child Boy - March 5th 1886 -

705 Girl at John Reed's - prolonged
labor - 1st Child - Boy - March 16th 1886

706 Wife of James Calloway - prolonged
Child Boy - March 16th 1886.

707 Wife of J. Lovelace - natural -
Boy - March 21st 1886

708 Wife of Thos. D. Morrison -
natural - Boy March - 23 - 1886

709 Wife of M. Atkins - Child cross
ways - turned - did well - Boy April 12.

710. Wife of John Sydee - Boy
April 25th 1886

711 Wife of M. E. Weaver - Girl
May 9th 1886

712 Wife of Wesley Roberts - Boy -
May 11th 1886.

713 Wife Chiney of Robert
Child girl June 22nd 86

714 Wife Horace Carter
Girl - June 23 - 1886

715 Wife Benj Burce
Girl June 29th 1886

716 Wife of [redacted] protracted
Child a boy

717 Wife of Lip Coleman, Placenta
Previa - child died - girl

718 Wife of Rufus Mann - natural
child Boy

719 Wife of Douglas Weaver - natural
child Boy Nov 21st 1886

720 Wife of J. J. Reagan - Child's
Cross wise - Boy. Nov 26th Jany 4

721 Wife of T. M. Garrison
Dec 1886

722 Wife of R. H. Weaver

723 Wife of J. Capps

724 Wife of Logan

725 Wife of George Peck

726 Daughter of Berry Bowen
May 10th 1887

727 - Wife of Mc Buckner
Girl May 19th 1887

728 Wife of A. S. Weaver
girl May 24th 1887

729 Wife of F. P. Roberts
Child girl May 26th 1887

730 Wife of A. Green - prol. child
Aug 18th 1886

731 Wife of Thos. L. Weaver
water broke in advance 36 hours
child a girl

732 Wife of C. A. Nichols -
child girl

733 Wife of C. P. Weaver
child girl - Aug 23rd 1887

734 - Wife of R. M. Williams
Natural Boy
Aug 30th 1887

Wife of Wolly Gill -
735 Natural - Girl - Dec 27th

Wife of Robt Black - natural
738 Girl - Jan 11th 1888 -

Wife of Benj. F. Morris
739 Natural - Girl - Feb 3rd 88

740 Wife of Mr Roberts -
Girl Jan 2nd 1888

741 Wife of Sam Clark natural
Girl Feb 1st 1888 did well

742 Wife of Benj Morris natural
girl did well - Feb 10th '88

Placenta retained
743 Wife of Dr. Rogers - Girl Feb 10th

How to Cure a felon.

Take Common Salt, roasted on a hot Stove until all the Chlorine is gone, or it is dry. Take 1 teaspoon full of this also
1 tea spoon full pulv. Castile Soap -
1 " " " Venice Turpentine -
Make a poultice, of them and apply to felon - Renew twice a day. In 4 Day it will be gone.

744 Wife of Josiah Lewis – Placenta retained – child girl – died well Feb 23

745 Wife of Mr. Fletcher
natural child Boy – Feb. 25 – 1888

747 wife of W. M. Sharp – child
twins – saved both – girl – March 14
1888

---

2 Tinct Lobelia 5 oz.
Amonia Iodide 2 Drachms
Amonia Bromide 3 "
Syrup of Tolulant 3 oz.
Sig. Tea Spoon full evy 1-2-3-&4 hours.

Asthma
Grindelia 8 Drachms
Jaborandi 8 "
Eucalyptus 4 "
Digitalis 4 "
Cubebs 4 "
Stramonium 16 "
Nitrate Potash 12 "
Cascarilla Bark 1 "
All Pulv. Burn & inhale. ¼ at a time.

Ammonia treatment of Typhoid fever

1 When high fever - give Nitrate of Ammonia 10 to 12 gr. doses, till temperature is reduced

2 When Diarrhea supervenes give Acetate of ammonia - Opium & Acetate of Lead

3 When nervous Symptoms supervene - tongue dry - teeth coated with sordes, give Carb. Ammonia & chlorate potash.

4 Should Coma occur give Hydrochlorate of Ammonia

Asthma

R	Tinct. Lobelia	5 ozs
	Iodide of Ammonia	2 Drachms
	Bromide of Ammonia	3 "
	Syrup of Tolu	3 oz

Dose 1 tea spoon full - every 1 - 2 - 3 hours

---

776 Wife of Joseph [illegible] Natural - Girl - March [illegible]

777 Wife of Gill White - Puerperal Eclampsia - Turned & delivered - Child alive - woman doing well

March 30th 88

Wizzard Oil. So called

Tinct Capsicum	℥ii
- Oil Sassafras	℥ii
Spirits Camphor (Alcoholic)	℥ii
Tinct Guaiac	℥ii
- Oil of Hemlock	℥ii
Aqua Amonia	℥iv
- Ether Sulph	℥iii
Alcohol	One gallon

Mix Thoroughly and bottle in
6 oz Bottles -

Menorrhagia

Tinct. Cannabis Indica	30 Drops
Pulveris tragac. Co	1 Drachm
Spiritus Chlorof.	1 "
Aqua	2 Oz

One ʒ every 3 hours.

(778) - wife of George Robeson
Child died - Syphilitic
March 30th 1888

Goiter

R Acetate Morphia 8 grains
Iodide mercury 6 "
Lard 1 oz.
apply night & morning - rub with hard substance - Egg, or Bone.
apply heat to produce absorption

Neuralgic Rheumatism

R. Licorice Root - Pulv. 110 grains
Sulph. Atropia 10 "
Sugar of Milk 1 oz.
Dose 5 grs. with ½ gr. Morphia

Tetter

R Alum 210 grains
Borax 200 "
Sugar of lead 40 "
Blue Vitriol 20 "
Rain Water 1 pint
Shake well - wash the parts
2 or 3 times a day

(780) Wife of Jas. Lowlace - matured
Boy - April 13 - '88

(676) Wife of M. A. Baird Nevada - 4 weeks before delivery - Sid awhile when full time came - Boy - April 12th 88

Dropsy

℞. ℥ss Acetate Potash
℥viii Infusion Digitalis
℥ii Tinct Cinnamon
Dose 1 or 2 drachms every
4 hours.

Corns

℞ ℥ii Strong apple vinegar
Bread Crumbs sufficient
Let stand till disolved
Apply as a Poultice on retiring
to bed. One or 2 applications are

Hoarseness

℞ Tinct. Chl. of Iron	2 drachms	
Glycerine	4	"
Aqua	4	"

Dose ½ tea spoon full frequently
repeated

Strangulated Hernia

℞ ℥v Ether poured on the tightly
stretched Skin in 15 minutes
in 1 hour the bowels will
replace themselves

Injection for Chordee
R. Potassa Bromidi ʒi ss
Tinct Opii ʒss
Glycerine ʒiii
Aqua ʒv.
four times daily – let remain for some 15 minutes.

Liniment.

Chloroform	2 ounces
Alcohol	2 "
Aqua Ammonia	2 "
Tinct Camphor	2 "
Tinct Aconite Root	2 "
Spts. Nit. Ether	6 "

McDade's treatment of Syphilis
Fl. Ext. Sarsaparilla
" " Queens Delight
" " Burdock
" " Polk root
" " Prickley ash – 1 tea spoon full
3 Times a day – increase the dose.

(7-81) Wife of Lee Coolin of Caledonia – She came for me [illegible] – to me at confinement and [illegible] a child was 44 years old and never [illegible] Birth April 25–88

To destroy Warts &c

R Acid Chromici 60 grs.
Aqua 4 Drachms
Paint lightly on Surface

In Hemorrhage in Typhoid fever

Oil Turpentine 10 Drops
Laudanum 10 "
Mucilage Acacia 4 Drachms
Water 1 oz
at once – every 3 hours.

Quinine Pills

R Sulph Quinine 20 grs.
Tartaric acid 4 "
Water 2 Drops

Leucorrhea

R. Fowler's Solution 6 drops 3 times a day = Cures in 10 days.

Diarrhoea & Dysentary

R. Ext. Blackberry root 3 Drachms
Aro. Syrup Rhubarb & Pot 1 oz
Ext. Hamamelis 3 Drachms
Tinct Opii. 2 "
One tea spoon full evry two or three hours – in water

Head ache

R. Hyd: Chloral 10 grs
Potas Bromide 20 "
Tinct. Gelsemii 30 drops
Aqua 1 oz

One tea spoon full evry 15 minutes

Tetanus

R Alcohol 1 part - Ether 2 - Chloroform 3
inhale to anesthesia is complete,

Catarrh of Bladder

R. Spts, Nit, Dulc 1 oz
Pulv. Gum acacia 1 "
Paregoric 1 "
Tinct Gelsemii. 1 drachm

One Tea spoon full evry 2 hours.

Tonic aperient Pills

Ext. Nux, Vomica 1/3 grain
" Hyosciami 1/2 "
Compound Colocynth 2 grs.

Pruritis Pudendi

R Sulph Soda ℨi } Mix
Aqua ℨiii } apply
Glycerine ℨi } frequently

Nasal Catarrh

℞ Acid Borate 1 drachm
Pulv Ulmus B " 3
Zinci Sulph 6 grs.
Pulv. Belladonna 10 grs.
To be Snuffed up Nose.

Irritibility of Bladder

℞ Ext. Belladonna 6 grs
" Hyoscyamus 12 "
Morphia Sulph 1 "
6 pills – one evy 4 or 6 hours

Nasal Catarrh

℞ Acid Cabolic 5 parts
Alcohol 15 "
Aqua Amonia 6 "
Aqua pure 10 "
Put in a dark wide-glass stopper
smell evy 2 or 3 hours.

℞ Carbolic acid ½ drachm
Acetic acid 2 ʒ
Water 6 ʒ
Oil Bergamot 10 drops

a Sure cure for Itch!

Quinine Pills

R Sulph. Quinine 20 grs.
Tartaric acid 4 "
Water 2 drops.

For Worms

R Calomel 8 grs
Soda Bi carb 8 "
Santonine 8 "
Rhubarb 8 "
Make 4 powders – one every Six Hours –

Flatulent Dyspepsia

R. Potass. Chlor. 2½ drachms
Soda Bi carb. 2½ "
Pulv. Rheub ½ "
" Capsic 4 grs.
Oil Sassafras 2 drops
Water ½ pint
One Table spoon full after each meal –

Tinea Capitis

R. Nit Silver 1 scruple
Red ox. Mercury 2 "
Iodide Lead 1 drachm
Cerate 2 "
Vaseline 2 "
Apply night & morning

Tonic Pills

R. Ext. Nux vomica 15 grs.
Ext. Valerian 20 "
Ext. Borosmia 20 "
Ext. Podophyllin 15 "
Iodide Manganese 20 "

Mix – make 30 pills.

one 3 times a day. in debility

Hair Dye

1/4 oz. Acetate Lead
1 oz. Glycerine
1/4 oz. Lac Sulphur
1 drachm oil Bergamot
12 oz. Rain Water

Diphtheria – Treatment

℞ Sodae, hyposulphite ʒviij
Aqua, distil ℥iij
Syr. simp

Sig. one half teaspoonful to a child eight months to one year old

Children
Summer Bowel Disease

℞ Tinct Opii XVI Gtt.
Sub. Nit. Bismuth ʒii
Syrup Simple ℥ss
Misturae Cretae ℥iss
Mix - Shake - Dose for infant 6 months old ½ tea spoon full evy 3 hours - 1 year - 1 tea spoon full

Inflamation of Colon

℞ ʒii Sub. Nit. Bismuth
℥i. Tinct. Opii
ʒi. Galic acid
℥i. Alcohol
℥ss. Ext. Cloves - fluid.
℥ss. Carb. Magnisia
℥viii. aqua. dist
Dose 1 to 2 tea spoons full evy 4 hours.

780 - Wife of John [illegible] - Colored - Boy - April 13th 1888

R Old Cough

Take Balm of Gilead buds make a strong tea - drink freely each night on going to bed

Scroffula - Salve for

R White pine Turpentine
Old Soft Soap
Bees wax
Sheep Suet - Equal parts of all

Stew it seven hours very slowly - Keep it close covered - in an earthen vessel - When done apply it on a piece of Broad cloth and apply to abscess - Keep it on 24 hours at a time &c

Corned Beef

To 100 lbs Beef - 6 gals. Soft Water - 9 lbs Salt - 3 lbs Brown Sugar - 1 quart Molasses - 2 oz Salt Peter - 1 oz pepper Red - 1 oz Potash Boil 15 Minutes - let cool - pour over the meat till it covers it well. Let stand - It will keep all year.

Neuralgic Pill

℞ Zinc Cyanuretum ... VI grs.
Quinine Sulph ... IX "
Morphia " ... ½ "
Ext. Belladona ... III grs.
Mix into six pills
One evy 6 hours.

Parsons Purgative Pills

℞ Powdered Soct. Aloes ... 1. gr
Hyd. Sub. Mur. ... ½ gr
Colocynth ... ¼ "
Gamboge ... ¼ "
Mandrake ... ½ "
Sapo. Hiss ... ¼ "
Ol. Menth. Pip ... ½ gtt.
The above makes one 3 gr pill
2 is a medium dose

℞ Bowel disease
1 Drachm Aromatic Syrup Rhubarb
10 grs. Soda
20 drops deodorized opium
3 times a day

℞. For Cancers
1 gr. Arsenous acid
2 Scruples pulv. Hyosciamus
Rub together and apply or sprinkle on
℞ Give Fowler's Solution in large doses
at the same time

For Syphilis
℞ 4 grs of Corrosive Sublimate
2 oz water,
Dose 1 drach 3 times a day & wash
the Chancres with Solution Sulph.
Copper — 10 grs. to the ℥ —

Cough Mixture
℞ Scaley Barked Hickory out side bark
Life-ever-lasting often in mixtures
Spikenard root. — Heart leaves — equal
quantities of each — 1/4 as much Cumfrey
root as of either — Boil each seperately
then mix and boil down — add honey to make
Syrup — to each quart of Syrup add one
table spoon full Sol. Amonia. 1 drach Elixir
vitriol. — 1 tea spoon full Benzoic acid
Dose 1 table spoon full 4 times a day

If it effects the head lessen dose.
For Bronchitis to the above add one table spoon full Tincture Capsicum

To take out Splinters & Thorns
℞ Make a plaster of Turpentine & Tallow - spread on leather, and apply to wound

Diarrhea & Flux
℞ Fill a cup 1/3 full of good apple vinegar put in salt as long as it will desolve - then fill the cup with boiling water - let it stand till cool, often stiring well - Dip of Skum - take 1 tablespoon full 3 times a day.

Hoarseness
℞ Take the whites of 2 eggs - Beat with 2 spoon fulls of white sugar - grate some nutmeg - then add a pint of warm water - Stir well - drink often & repeat if necessary.

Thrush & Sore Mouths
℞ apply Sulph Ether once a day with a Camel hair pencil

Hydrophobia
℞ Fill the wound with Pulv. Lunar Costic as soon as possible.

Cancers

R Chloride of Zink & Pulverized Blood Root. The zink is rubbed with the root until a past is formed without adding any fluid - Spread on Cloth just the size of the canser - remain on 24 hours - ~~wait~~ five days and apply again &c.

Gonorrhea

R Equal quantities of Burdock Root - Polk Root & Queen of the meadow Boil to one quart - put in 1 gal water 1 table spoon full 3 times a day.

Cough

R Equal parts of Sulphur & Alum & sufficient quantity of Tar - make pills Take 2 at night & one of a morning

---

- for Bad Vaccinated arms Bathe in Coal oil three times a day.

Bone fellon

A Poultice of Onions applied three times a day for 3 or 4 days.

Substitute for Borax

℞ 3 lbs Salt
1 lb. Copperas
15 lbs Sharp Sand – Mix and use as Borax.

Asthma

℞ The white & Shell of Six eggs.
1 pt. apple vinegar – put them in an earthen vessel, and sink in the ground for 48 or 60 hours – take it out and add
1 pt. Good apple Brandy
½ pt Honey – Let it stand for 24 hours. Dose 1 table spoonfull 3 times a day.

Old Sore Leggs.

℞ 1 fl. Oz Spirits of Harts horn
½ oz Camphor – Gum
½ pt. Lard – Simmer together and bathe once a day

Tooth Ache

½ oz Chloroform – 30 grs Tannin
Saturate Cotton and fill cavity

Morning Sickness in Pregnancy

℞ 10 to 20 grs of Cascarilla

For Itch

℞ ℥i Sublimed Sulphur
℥viii Quick lime
℥x Water = Boil till mixed and apply to the skin

Milk for Sucking Children

℞ Oi ~~Water~~ Cow's milk
℥ss Sugar
℥iii Water = nearly woman's milk

Test for mucus and puss.

℞ act on it with Costic Potash if it dissolves it is mucus & if it forms ropy mass it is puss.

Diarrhea & bowel Complaints

℞ ℥i chloroform
℥ii Pulverized Cloves
℥ii Pulverized Cinnamon
℥ii Ipecacuanha
Oi old whisky – well shaken

Dose for Adults 1 table spoonful, dilute with water –

Tomatto Wine

R Take ripe Tomatoes, pick off the stems put them into a tub wash them clean - then strain through a linen bag. (1 bushel makes 6 gal.) add 3 lbs loaf sugar to each gal. then put into a cask, and ferment, and fix as rasp berry wine;

Blackberry Wine

R

Put the berries in a vessel and mash well - let them ferment for 12 hours. - then strain & to every 3 qts. of juice add 3 lbs. of brown sugar & 1 qt. of water. Stir it well together - then let it stand and ferment - taking off the froth often until fermentation ceases which will be about 20 hours - Then strain carefully taking out all sediment - Place in close vessels (demijohns or jugs) cork and keep till March

---

For Tetter

R Equal parts of

Cast Steal Soap

Cedament of Colibiate water &

fresh Butter - apply as ointment

℞

5 Snake Bite – mad dog – Spider &c
℞ Spts. Amonia applyed to the bite
and taken, diluted, inwardly

---

(1) For Blenorargia
℞ Not used in the inflamatory stage
4 oz Cubebs & 1 oz alum – made in
20 doses – one to be given every three
hours
(2) ℞ 1 oz Cubebs – 1 oz Balsam Copabia
1 oz of Burned Magnesia. 1 Scruple at
a dose three times per day.
(3) ℞ 1 oz Copabia – ½ drachm oil of cubebs
– 6½ drachms oil Turpentine – 1 oz Sweet
Spirits of niter – 2 oz ginger Syrup
give from 1 to 2 tea spoonfulls three times
a day – Shake well before using – good
also in gleet.

For Injections in same
(1) ℞ ½ oz Copavia – 3 oz musylage
used 3 times per day

(2) ℞ 1 Scruple sugar of lead – 1 Scruple Sulphate of Zink – 6 oz water – use a glass syringe – give 5 or 6 times per day always after making water.

(3) ℞ 10 to 20 grs tanic acid – 6 oz of water

(4) ℞ 10 grs Chloride of Zink = 20 grs. tanic acid & 8 oz water

(5) ℞ 1/4 to 1/2 nitrate of silver to 1 oz water.

Hope's mixture

℞ ʒi nitric acid.
℥viii Camphor water
40 gtt Tincture of opium
take one to 3 drachms.

Cough mixture

℞ ℥v decoction of Senega
℥ss Syrup of tulo
ʒii Paregoric
ʒii ~~Tincture~~ Tincture of Squills
℈i Carbonate of Amonia
take one table spoon full – good in Chronic Bronchetis

For Gastric Vertigo

R Argenti Oxidi 1/4 gr

Pulv. Capsici 1/4 ″

Ext. Colocyn Co. 1 ″

Pulv. Gum Camph 1/2 ″

M. ft. Pil. No 1 after each meal

For Hemorrhage – lungs &c

R Fl. Ext. Ipecac 5 drops

Tinct Digitalis 10 ″

Fl. Ext. Ergot 1 Drachm

Repeat as required

Receipts

1 Dropsy — ½ ℥ Muriate of Iron 1/4 ℥. Spts. Niter. 1 drachm of Balsom Copabia — give as circumstances require.

---

2 Ulcers — Copperas pulverized 9 mixed with Sweet Lard

---

3 Piles. Set in Cold water twice daily ½ hour — & use the ointment above for ulcers

---

4 Cough — 1 part opium — 2 parts Camphire — 3 parts Casteal Soap — mix thoroughly — Dose 1 grain on going to bed.

---

5 Dispepsia — 5 grains Quinine — 3 ℈ gr. H. Acid — 5 gr. Rhubarb — S. Carb. Soda 2 ʒ — Annise Seed 2 ʒ — Water 15 ℥ — give as may be required

Dose Typhoid fever [illegible]

Iodine 8 grains

Iodide Potas 30 grs

Water 1/2 ℥

Do 15 drops in water every

2 or 3 hours

Sciatica

℞ Balsam Copabia - 4 ℥

Tinct Laudanum - 4 drachms

" Hyosiami - ʒ "

Bi-carb pot - 1 -

Mucilage - 1 ℥

Aqua - 6 -

Dose 1 Table spoon full every

4 hours.

—Louisville Medical Review

RESTORATION OF THE MENSES.—*Editor Med. Brief:* For the benefit of Dr. S. W. Hopkins, I give the following recipe for the restoration of the menses, when stopped by cold or exposure, which I have never known to fail:

℞.—	Gum Guaiac.	℥ ij.
	Balsam Canadensis	℥ ii.
	Oil Sassafras	ʒ ij.
	Corrosive Sublimate	grs. xx.
	Alcohol	℥ viij.

Sig.: Twenty drops in wine glass of water night and morning, commencing ten days before expected time.

Dissolve the guaiac. and balsam in one-half of the alcohol, and corrosive sublimate in the other half; let guaiac. and balsam digest for five or six days, then pour off the clear liquid and mix with the corrosive sublimate and add the oil sassafras.

EXCELSIOR
TRADE MARK
WARRANTED
THIS CERTIFIES THAT THE ACCOMPANYING CASE No. IS MADE OF TWO SOLID PLATES OF GOLD COVERING A PLATE OF HARD COMPOSITION.
GUARANTEED TO WEAR FOR 20 YEARS.

EXCELSIOR
TRADE MARK
WARRANTED
THIS CERTIFIES THAT THE ACCOMPANYING CASE No. IS MADE OF TWO SOLID PLATES OF GOLD COVERING A PLATE OF HARD COMPOSITION.
GUARANTEED TO WEAR FOR 20 YEARS.

HARTLEY'S SUPERIOR HAIR RESTORER RECIPE.

———oo———

¼ oz. Sugar of Lead.

1 oz. Glycerine.

¼ oz. Lac Sulphur.

3 gills Rain Water.

One ¼ dram Oil of Bergamot.

———oo———

How to Prepare It.

Take a pint bottle and fill it three-quarters full of pure rain water. Cover the bottle completely with paper, to exclude the light. Then add the other ingredients; let it stand for about twenty four hours, and it is ready for use. Many object to the sediment caused by the Sulphur. That can be avoided by first placing the s[illegible] water together and letting them stand for a c[illegible] as much as seems possible of the sulphur [illegible] and add the other ingredients. Be pa[illegible]r, and not Flowers of Sulphur.

INDEX

Index of names given by Dr. Reagan, number he assigned, and date of visit.

Carter, Ashbell, 492 (6/18/79)
Horace 714 (6/23/86)
Chambers, Jacob 590 (5/13/82)
Joseph 169 (9/12/66), 191 (8/29/67), 225 (11/12/68), 227 (11/13/68), 609 (10/13/82)
Chambers, Joseph 691 (10/11/85)
Chandler, Elijah 54 (4/24/61)
Cheek, W. B. 2 (9/8/58), 35 (11/5/60), 93 (5/1/63)
Clark, Elisha 170 (9/26/66), 250 (10/16/69), 316 (2/22/72)
Sam 741 (2/1/88)
Wm., Jr. 461 (8/7/78)
Clinton, W. 173 (11/7/66)
W. T. 359 (4/3/74)
Clontz, Dr. W. J. 680 (4/28/85)
William 100 (6/26/63)
Cole, James 178 (1/13/67)
Joseph 402 (8/4/76)
Coleman, Isaac 486 (4/17/79), 606 (8/25/82)
Lip 717 (Summer 1886)
Miles 181 (6/2/67)
W. 22 (1/21/60)
Colfee, J. H. 82 (12/6/62)
John A. 55 (6/22/61)
Colper, J. H. 226 (11/5/68)
Conner, W. O. 616 (11/20/82)
Cook, D. A. 11 (3/28/59)
James 557 (7/22/81)
Newton 558 (7/30/81)
W. B. 33 (8/9/60)
Corbin, Lee 781 (4/25/88)
Corbit, Wm. 450 (3/7/78)
Cosby, J. M. 603 (8/13/82)
Crage, Bob 639 (8/23/83)
Crecy, Wm. 161 (6/27/66)
Crook, J. 630 (3/23/82)
Mr. 553 (6/11/81)
Curtis, Ashbell 407 (8/25/76)
Davis, James 197 (1/16/68), 252 (10/25/69)
John 647 (1/10/84), 678 (3/18/85)
Thos. 685 (6/3/85)
William 152 (3/20/66), 273 (1/30/71)
Wm. M. 554 (6/15/89)
Rev. W. P. 663 (4/27/84)
Douriaboo, Jef. 700 (2/25/86)
Draper, Thos. 237 (2/17/69)
Dula, Rev. J. M. 332 (9/8/72)
Edmonds, Miss Polly 210 (7/10/68)
Tilman 309 (12/25/71)
Edmonds, W. R. 166 (8/20/66), 258 (1/9/70)
Wm. 262 (6/26/70)
Edwards, Allen 168 (9/13/66)
Henry N. 49 (3/22/61)
James 221 (9/4/68), 281 (6/25/71)
Matt. 400 (7/5/76)
Thos. 495 (8/9/79), 571 (1/27/82), 702 (3/11/86), 659 (3/26/84)
Tim. 365 (6/30/74)
Vol. 366 (7/6/74)
Wm. 512 (4/19/80)
Elkins, Gilbert 521 (4/5/80)
Jane 425 (5/7/77)
R. N. 485 (4/16/79)
Ellen, Miss (Negro) 214 (7/27/68)
Eller, Albert 550 (5/20/81), 650 (1/15/84), 695 (1/2/86)
J. H. 109 (3/7/64), 147 (2/10/66)
Miss Rebecca 190 (8/26 & 27/67)
Rev. J. P. 585 (5/4/82)
W. C. 305 (12/10/71)
Wisby 37 (12/16/60), 105 (11/18/63)
William 204 (5/3/68), 261 (4/9/70), 340 (Spring 1873)
Ellis, James H. 47 (3/10/61)
Wm. 266 (7/27/70)
English, John 440 (12/24/77)
Fagg, Col. John A. 215 (8/4/68)
Fair, A. D. 108 (2/29/64)
Marshal 442 (1/16/78), 646 (12/25/83)
Fair, Wm. 687 (7/24/85)
Farmer, Thos. J. 531 (12/22/80)
Flac, Rolf
Flack, Bruce 519 (6/29/80), 580 (3/19/82), 716 (Summer 1886)
Rob. 510 (4/4/80)
Roll 471 (11/15/78), 578 (3/18/82), 655 (1/23/84), 696 (1/2/86), 738 (1/10/88)
Fletcher, Mr. 745 (2/25/88)
Fore, Thos. 417 (12/22/75?)
Fox, A. M. 7 (Fall 1858), 78 (10/29/62)
Chris 651 (1/17/84)
Lafayette 79 (11/12/62)
Marion 26 (4/17/60), 116 (4/5/64)
Marshal 381 (6/4/75)
Frady, James 1 (8/31/58)
Framsworth, Wiley (colored) 516 (6/5/80)
Frazier, Rev. A. J. 437 (9/21/77)
Garrison, J. M. 312 (1/19/72), 335 (Winter 1872), 539 (1/31/81)
J. W. 235 (2/12/69)
James 374 (11/8/74, 377 (12/23/74), 415 (11/29/76)

Garrison, James M. 293 (9/16/71)
Mitchel 135 (10/14/65)
T. M. 289 (8/11/71), 331 (8/28/72), 361 (4/18/74), 439 (12/4/77), 501 (1/3/80), 592 (5/27/82), 720 (December 1886)
Thos. 115 (3/19/64), 294 (9/23/71)
W. C. 56 (6/25/61), 106 (12/1/63), 313 (1/22/72), 373 (9/1/74), 414 (11/20/76), 522 (4/5/80)
W. H. 69 (5/16/62)
Gentry, G. W. 395 (4/8/76)
Mrs. Myra 188 (8/15/67)
Joseph 184 (6/29/67), 594 (6/11/82)
Gibbs, Joshua 371 (8/26/74)
Gill, Wesley 411 (9/28/76), 483 (4/1/79), 564 (9/19/81), 672 (12/18/84), 735 (12/27/87)
A. J., Black girl of, 19 (12/14/59)
Goodson 329 (7/20/72)
Green, A. 730 (8/18/87)
Griffin, Walker 286 (7/25/71)
Grolsly, E. M. 447 (2/26/78)
Gunty, G. W. 155 (3/30/66)
Gutherie, Thos. 535 (1/10/81)
Guty, Newt 341 (5/1/73)
Newton 165 (8/15/66)
Gwaltney, J. A. 552 (6/6/81), 617 (11/25/82), 648 (1/11/84), 689 (9/3/85)
Jesse 468 (10/12/78)
Hamilton, Hughey 171 (9/29/66), 216 (8/17/68), 308 (12/13/71), 342 (6/3/73)
Wm. 641 (9/18/83)
Hampton, George 424 (5/3/77)
James 549 (4/24/81)
Turly 39 (12/26/60)
Haren, Charles 693 (12/24/85)
J. M. 128 (4/25/65)
Judson 457 (6/18/78)
Madison 92 (4/8/63)
W. J. 25 (4/4/60)
Harris, Charles 654 (1/22/84)
Dr. 172 (10/23/66)
Dr. J. A. 347 (9/24/73), 530 (12/17/80)
Isaiah 287 (8/3/71)
Madison 185 (7/16/67)
Hembree, James 355 (3/8/74), 484 (4/5/79), 614 (11/12/82)
Henderson, John 370 (8/25/74), 404 (8/18/76), 464 (9/21/78), 523
Henderson, John (7/19/80), 573 (2/23/82), 667 (6/15/84), 703 (3/14/86)
Henly, James 403 (8/8/76)
Henry, Lee 428 (7/16/77)
Holt, Jackson 322 (6/4/72)
Hooker, H. 379 (4/16/75)
Howard, Nineva 494 (8/8/79), 584 (4/20/82), 633 (5/1/83)
Huff, Lem 318 (3/25/72), 353 (2/25/74)
Len 418 (1/23/77), 498 (9/26/79), 671 (12/9/84)
Hughey, Willis 88 (3/6/63)
Hughs, John 251 (10/17/69), 545 (3/29/81)
Lee 701 (2/27/86)
Hughy, Chrisly 302 (12/3/71)
Hunsucker, D. 177 (1/9/67), 251 (10/21/69)
Hunter, Jack 480 (2/4/79), 567 (11/4/81)
W. H. 528 (12/8/80), 576 (3/9/82)
Hyatt, Lucinda 50 (3/30/61)
Isreal, Col. J. M., Servant girl of, 80 (11/12/62)
Jenkins, Henry 194 (9/11/67)
John 292 (8/30/71)
Jenkins, Washington 21 (1/5/60), 117 (7/13/64), 145 (1/28/66), 187 (8/12/67)
William, Jr. 208 (6/11/68)
Wm. 36 (11/22/60)
Jennings, William 113 (3/15/64)
Jinney, Negro girl 151 (3/2/66)
Johnson, Lem 674 (1/21/85)
Joiner, Henry 481 (2/21/79)
James 540 (2/11/81), 608 (10/2/82), 670 (9/10/84)
Rev. E. H. 278 (5/8/71)
Jones, Elias 174 (11/13/66)
John 397 (5/19/76), 458 (7/17/78)
Matt 144 (January 1866)
Rev. E. H. 345 (8/17/73)
Rev. Elias 81 (12/5/62)
W. W. 61 (8/14/61), 242 (4/12/69)
William 143 (January 1866)
Joyner, James 467 (9/27/78)
Jump, Wm. 239 (3/14/69)
Justice, George 284 (7/17/71)
Rev. Amos 568 (12/26/81)
Keever, Milton 180 (5/13/67)
Keigler, J. W. 317 (3/5/72)
Keith, Arnold 211 (7/11/68), 474 (12/2/78)
J. A. 386 (8/18/75)
James 577 (3/17/82)
Kerr, Samuel 254 (3/6/74)
Kever, Milton 644 (10/16/83)
Kiegler, Wm. 268 (8/1/70)

Kiever, Milton 231 (1/5/69)
Kiger, Chrisly 306 (12/11/71)
Joseph 183 (6/22/67)
Kigler, J. W. 224 (10/31/68)
Wm. 160 (5/23/66)
Kirkendall, Wm. 699 (2/5/86)
Kizer, Joseph 257 (12/25/69), 320 (5/1/72)
Lea, Mrs. 315 (2/20/72)
Lankford, Andrew 44 (2/17/61)
Jordan 4 (9/21/58)
Lassiter, Wm. 263 (7/7/70)
Litteral, Can 230 (1/2/69)
Thos. 12 (5/1/59), 48 (3/17/61)
Logann 724 (No Date)
Lovelace, J. 707 (3/21/86)
John 660 (4/16/84), 780 (4/13/88)
Mr. 595 (6/24/82)
Lydee, John 710 (4/25/86)
Mackey, Logan 514 (5/4/80), 586 (5/5/82)
Macky, J. J. 275 (2/27/71)
Marten, Rev. John 574 (3/4/82)
Martin, Albert 636 (5/31/83)
Marion 623 (1/2/83)
Maulden, Miss Angeline 13 (5/25/59)
McAbee, Berry 497 (9/12/79), 559 (8/3/81)
Henry 570 (1/21/82)
John 324 (6/26/72)
McAlpine, A. J. 247 (6/25/69), 307 (12/12/71)
McCehine, Miss Ann 157 (4/15/66)
McIntyre, Barnett 323 (6/22/72)
McKinney, Charles 62 (12/5/61), 95 (5/30/63), 264 (7/9/70), 283 (7/13/71)
Moore, E. W., Rev. 87 (2/15/63)
Joseph 469 (10/20/78), 515 (5/5/80), 560 (8/5/81)
Morehead, Bob 581 (4/2/82)
Morris, Benj. 742 (2/10/88)
Benj. F. 739 (2/3/88)
Thos. 16 (7/30/59)
Morrison, Thos. S. 626 (2/9/83), 708 (3/23/86)
Munday, Alex, Negro girl of, 63 (12/12/61)
Mundy, Calvin 220 (9/4/68)
Myers, Joseph 234 (2/6/69)
Nelan, Miss Matilda 285 (7/20/71)
Nelson, Capt. J. B. 90 (3/26/63)
Newton, Alford 605 (8/22/82)
Nichols, C. A. 337 (Spring 1873),
Nichols, C. A. 355 (7/12/75), 432 (9/9/77), 505 (2/17/80), 635 (5/24/83)
C. N. 732 (August 1887)
John A. 504 (1/31/80)
Palmer, Joseph 776 (3/9/88)
Parham, Joseph 694 (12/25/85)
Paris, J. F. 490 (5/25/79)
Parker, Benjamin 30 (6/8/60)
Capt. 103 (9/9/63)
Henry (Negro) 213 (7/19/68), 496 (8/22/79)
James 112 (2/28/64)
R. W., Rev. 60 (7/20/61)
Shipley 677 (3/10/85)
Thos. 83 (12/10/62), 176 (12/21/66), 228 (12/3/68)
W. F., Rev. 6 (Fall 1858), 45 (2/27/61), 431 (9/6/77)
W. F., Negro girl of, 59 (7/17/61)
Parris, J. F. 541 (2/12/81)
John 543 (2/28/81), 621 (12/22/82)
Patten, J. W. 398 (5/20/76)
Patterson, J. R. 236 (2/13/69)
Peace, James 396 (4/22/76), 456 (4/28/78), 563 (9/18/81), 681 (5/6/85)
Peak, George 460 (8/2/78), 612 (10/28/82), 725 (No Date)
Jackson 463 (8/13/78)
Pegram, Arthur 593 (6/1/82)
Penix, Wm. 610(10/14/82)
Penland, Burton 392 (2/7/76)
Chrisley 310 (12/25/71), 679 (4/14/85)
James 562 (8/26/81), 697 (1/25/85)
Lee 390 (1/7/76)
Robert 222 (10/1/68)
Pennix 364 (6/24/74)
Philips, Joe 566 (October 1881)
Pickens, Bill (colored) 551 (5/24/81)
Rev. R. W. 89 (3/19/63), 124 (2/21/65), 179 (1/20/67), 274 (1/31/71)
Will 686 (6/20/85)
Ponder, Rev. Frank 453 (4/1/78), 485 (4/8/79)
Pope, Rev. T. J. 255 (12/14/69)
Priscilla, a negro girl 156 (4/13/66)
Ramsey, 602 (7/27/82)
Robert 175 (11/15/66)
Wiley 419 (1/23/77)
Ray, Col. J. M. 121 (12/11/64)
Erving 351 (2/8/74)
Kelsey 52 (4/15/61)
Moore 430 (8/23/77)
William 413 (11/5/76), 448 (2/27/78)
Reagan, D. H. 344 (8/14/73), 401 (8/4/76), 493 (7/5/79)
J. J. 20 (1/3/60), 74 (7/28/62),

www.ingramcontent.com/pod-product-compliance
Lightning Source LLC
Chambersburg PA
CBHW080626030426
42336CB00018B/3096
9781639140725